Mississippi Musicians Hall of Fame

Legendary Musicians Whose Art Has Changed the World

Edited by James H. Brewer

QUAIL RIDGE PRESS
Brandon, Mississippi

Copyright ©2001 by Mississippi Musicians Hall of Fame
All Rights Reserved

No part of this book may be reproduced or utilized in any form or by any means, electronic or mechanical, including photocopying and recording, or by any information storage and retrieval system, without permission in writing from the publisher.

Cover art by Liz Bass
Printed in Canada

ISBN 1-893062-20-1

Mississippi Musicians Hall of Fame is a 501-c-3 non-profit organization.
Proceeds support the Mississippi Musicians Hall of Fame.
P. O. Box 1270 • Clinton, MS 39060 • 601-924-0131 • www.msmusic.org

---

Library of Congress Cataloging-in-Publication Data

Mississippi musicians hall of fame : legendary musicians whose art has changed the world / edited by James H. Brewer.
    p. cm.
  Includes bibliographical references and index.
  ISBN 1-893062-20-1
    1. Musicians—Mississippi—Biography—Dictionaries. I. Brewer, James H. II. Mississippi Musicians Hall of Fame.
ML106.U4 M6 2001
780'.92'2762—dc21
[B]   00-045957

QUAIL RIDGE PRESS
P. O. Box 123 • Brandon, MS 39043 • 1-800-343-1583
www.quailridge.com • info@quailridge.com

Table of Contents

Acknowledgments 4

Preface 5

Introduction 7

List of Charter Nominees and Inductees 10

Blues 13

Classical 43

Country Music 59

Gospel and Religious Music 85

Jazz 97

Motion Pictures and Television 119

Musical Theater, Broadway 125

Popular (Pop) 131

Production, Recording and Promotion 137

Rhythm and Blues, Soul 145

Rock and Roll 157

Mississippi Music Heritage Museum 167

References 168

Resources 169

Index 171

Acknowledgments

·····

This book is the result of assistance by many Mississippi musicians, historians, and music lovers. Hundreds of people furnished little-known facts or complete biographies about Mississippi's great musicians. Much information came from family members and not academic sources. Other information came from research on the internet and reference materials.

In addition, the selection of artists featured in this book was aided by a process conducted by the Mississippi Musicians Hall of Fame. Dr. Ellistine Holly chaired the selection committee. The committee members surveyed a group of nationally known music historians and experts. This survey resulted in a list of fifty-seven potential nominees and inductees for the Mississippi Musicians Hall of Fame. That information and research was used in this book.

The many contributors and advisors for this book include: Gayle Dean Wardlow, blues; Dr. Antoinette Handy, black musicians; James L. Cox, research; Christine Wilson, Mississippi Department of Archives and History, advice; Nancy Jacobs, Starkville High School Writers and Musicians Project, editing and research; the students of Starkville High School's music project, research; The Mississippi State Department of Education, research and editing; John Morrow, Jim Buck Ross Agriculture and Forestry Museum, research; Judith Brewer, editing; Steve LaVere, Robert Johnson; David Weaver, Ruby Elzy; and The Mississippi Library Commission, research.

Thanks to the winners of the Mississippi Musicians Hall of Fame student writers contest for their contributions. State high school students were asked to research and write about Mississippi musicians. Some of their research is included in this book. The winners were Eun Oh Lee; Shanita Bishop; Ericka Mordecai; and first place winner, Nicole Rafferty. All of the research done by students was helpful.

Many thanks to the Mississippi Musicians Hall of Fame Board of Directors for their support: Dr. London Branch, Dr. Charles Elliott, Mr. Ronald Herrington, Dr. Ellistine Holly, Mr. Jerry Mannery, Mrs Ruth McWilliams, and Dr. Cora Norman. Any errors in this book, if they exist, are my fault, not theirs.

Jim Brewer

Preface

Mississippi Musicians Hall of Fame: Legendary Musicians Whose Art Has Changed the World adds to the growing realization that Mississippi is the birthplace of America's music.

A Californian, Steve Russell, said, "Mississippi should be declared a national monument for all the musicians it has produced." Mississippi musicians have more than proven their talents to the world. It is time we recognize their contribution.

Mississippi musicians are known the world over. Yet few realize these talented artists are Mississippi natives. For hundreds of years, great Mississippi musicians have made their marks in every musical genre.

America's unique musical art forms can be traced to post-slavery days with roots deep in the Mississippi Delta. It is ironic that out of this flat fertile land with its slavery, poverty, poor education, and oppression would come such a wonderful gift to the world, the blues. And later, from a sickly young man out of the hills of East Mississippi, would come the legacy of country music.

These early music types led to, or influenced, the development of rock and roll, rhythm and blues, rockabilly, gospel, jazz, and popular music. With music as their vehicle for mutual respect, blacks and whites in Mississippi learned from each other. They played and sang together while forming new expressions in style. Even in the early 1800s, the first American concert singer, who was black, was born in Mississippi. And so, Mississippi's music was more than entertainment; it was a way out and a way up. It was a way of survival. It is this state's history.

Introduction

The collective efforts and talents of the musicians featured in this book have made Mississippi the music state. Indeed, Mississippi is the birthplace of America's music and is recognized as such by many music historians and researchers. The real question is why, in one of the poorest states in the union, do you find such a rich musical history and heritage? It is because music in Mississippi is more than entertainment; it tells the story of a state's, and ultimately a nation's, people.

If we assume that the blues is the basis for today's popular music, then, again, we can assume that Mississippi is the birthplace of America's music. Alan Lomax in his book, *The Land Where the Blues Began,* said, "Although this has been called the age of anxiety, it might better be termed the century of the blues, after the moody song style that was born sometime around 1900 in the Mississippi Delta." Lomax goes on to credit black delta blues musicians by saying, "Their productions transfixed audiences, and white performers rushed to imitate and parody them in the minstrel show, buck dancing, ragtime, jazz, as nowadays in rock, rap, and the blues."

While there was indeed anxiety between blacks and whites in Mississippi, at least one venue demanded mutual respect—music. Robert M. Baker, author of "A Brief History of the Blues," quotes Joseph Machlis: ". . . blues is a native American musical and verse form, with no direct European and African antecedents of which we know. In other words, it is a blending of both traditions." However, there is no question that rhythmic dance tunes brought over by slaves influenced greatly the development of the blues. Blacks took the instruments and church music from Europe and wove them with their ancestral rhythms into what we know as the blues.

Christine Wilson, in the Mississippi Department of Archives and History publication *All Shook Up: Mississippi Roots of American Popular Music,* said, "Music that emerged from Mississippi has shaped the development of popular music of the country and world. Major innovators created new music in every form—gospel, blues, country, R&B, rock, and jazz."

William Ferris, in *Blues from the Delta,* wrote, "Blues shape both popular and folk music in American culture, and blues-yodeling Jimmie

Rodgers, Elvis Presley, and The Rolling Stones are among many white performers who incorporate blues in their singing styles."

For another example, Joachim Berendt's book, *The Jazz Book,* outlines the development of jazz from its blues roots. He indicates that folk blues led to classic blues, boogie, swing, bebop, Dixieland jazz, and to other forms of modern day jazz. Consequently, all of these jazz forms had their beginnings in the delta of Mississippi.

Although Charlie Patton may be the first folk blues artist to be recorded and recognized, he was not the first folk blues artist. That person is unknown. And while W. C. Handy may be called the Father of the Blues, he did not "invent" the blues. He said in his book, *Father of The Blues,* "Then one night at Tutwiler [Mississippi] . . . A lean, loose-jointed Negro had commenced plucking a guitar beside me while I slept. His song struck me instantly. . . . In this way, and from these materials, they set the mood for what we now call blues." From that experience, we know that W. C. Handy went on to compose and popularize the blues, thanks to that unknown folk blues artist in Tutwiler, Mississippi.

As blues developed in Mississippi after the 1900s into the 1920s, it began to emerge into the mainstream of popular music. For some time it had been described as the devil's music and was performed mostly in juke joints and local parties. Black and white musicians in Mississippi did things together in the 1920s that even in the 1960s would have been unheard of. Jimmie Rodgers, for example, invited Ishmon Bracey and Tommy Johnson, both black blues artists, to perform with him at the King Edward Hotel in Jackson. This was after Rodgers heard them playing on the street in front of the hotel. The blues influence on Jimmie Rodgers can be heard in many of his songs, such as *Train Whistle Blues* recorded in 1929.

In his book, *Elsie McWilliams, I Remember Jimmie,* Edward Bishop said of Jimmie Rodgers, ". . . the man who set the style of modern country music and who is looked upon as the most prominent pioneer in this field, is popularly called 'THE GREATEST COUNTRY ARTIST OF THEM ALL', was a Mississippian."

Jimmie Rodgers went on, of course, to be called the Father of Country Music. However, according to Gayle Dean Wardlow in his book, *Chasin' That Devil Music, Searching for the Blues,* Jimmie Rodgers came to Jackson in 1926 to record a demo tape for RCA Victor with then talent scout H. C. Speir. Speir had a music store on Farish Street and had discovered many great blues artists in the 1920s and 1930s. For that, he is called the Godfather of Delta Blues. But after hearing Rodgers play, Speir said, "Jimmie, you're not ready to record right now." Speir told Rodgers to go back to Meridian, work up some more songs, and come back later. Six months later, Rodgers found another way to get his songs on Victor. The rest is history. Jimmie Rodgers went on to be the first country singer inducted into the Country Music Hall of Fame. He is the only musician to be inducted into four different music halls of fame.

But blues and country are not the only genres to have their roots in Mississippi. The most influential figure in rock and roll music ever was Elvis Presley from Tupelo. Sam Phillips of Sun Records said that Elvis took from country, blues, white and black gospel, and western music and developed a new form of rock and roll. Elvis was greatly influenced by gospel singer James Blackwood and the Blackwood Brothers, also from Mississippi. However, Jackie Brenson of Clarksdale is said to have recorded the first true rock and roll recording, *Rocket 88*, in 1951.

The reader will discover throughout this book accounts of many musical firsts in Mississippi. Most of these "firsts" have led to significant contributions in the world of music. Moreover, the reader will discover that these legendary Mississippi musicians whose art has changed the world continue to make their marks. Mississippi musical artists continue to break sales records and to garner award after award. They are at the very top of every musical expression. They continue to be the kings, first ladies, godfathers, and fathers of all kinds of musical genres.

In an article in *The Clarion Ledger* on March 30, 2000, writer Donnie Snow summed it all up. "Mississippi is music. From Elvis Presley to Jimmie Rodgers to Robert Johnson, you'd be hard pressed to find some form of American music that can't find its history burgeoning either in the rich, dark Delta soil or under the warm Mississippi sun. Many around the world revere Mississippi as the holy land, and not because of the fine religious folk."

This book, with apologies, is not complete. It seems an impossible task to uncover and discover all the old and new musical talent from this state. As extensive as the research has been, not all deserving individuals will be included. Perhaps with the help of family and friends, any oversights will be corrected in future publications.

Jim Brewer

The First Mississippi Musicians Hall of Fame Induction Gala

On April 1, 2000, the first induction gala was held by the Mississippi Musicians Hall of Fame. Fifty-six great Mississippi musicians were nominated, and twenty-seven were inducted. Over 600 people from across the nation attended the gala. Each year this event will induct new members into the hall of fame and feature major musical entertainment.

The charter nominees and inductees from the first Mississippi Musicians Hall of Fame ceremony are listed on the following two pages.

•••••

Charter Nominees and Inductees
Inaugural Awards Induction • April 1, 2000
(Bold type indicates inductees)

BLUES
   PIONEER STATUS
     Son House • Coahoma County
     Robert Johnson • Hazlehurst
     Charlie Patton • Mississippi Delta
     Muddy Waters • Rolling Fork
   CONTEMPORARY STATUS
     B. B. King • Indianola
     Howlin' Wolf • White Station

CLASSICAL COMPOSERS
   PIONEER STATUS
     William Grant Still • Woodville
   CONTEMPORARY STATUS
     Samuel Jones • Inverness
     James Sclater • Clinton

CLASSICAL PERFORMERS
   PIONEER STATUS
     Ruby Elzy • Pontotoc
     Elizabeth Taylor Greenfield
     Natchez
   CONTEMPORARY STATUS
     John Alexander • Meridian
     Leontyne Price • Laurel

COUNTRY PERFORMERS
   PIONEER STATUS
     Jimmie Rodgers • Pine Springs
   CONTEMPORARY STATUS
     Faith Hill • Star
     Charley Pride • Sledge
     Conway Twitty • Friars Point
     Tammy Wynette • Tremont

B. B. King (right) accepts his Mississippi Musicians Hall of Fame award from Dr. Charles Elliott.

COUNTRY SONGWRITERS,
ARRANGERS, AND COMPOSERS
  PIONEER STATUS
    Elsie McWilliams • Harperville
  CONTEMPORARY STATUS
    Hank Cochran • Isola
    Ben Peters • Hollandale

GOSPEL AND RELIGIOUS
  PIONEER STATUS
    James Blackwood / Blackwood Brothers • Ackerman
    Five Blind Boys • Piney Woods School
    Pop Staples / Staples Singers • Drew
    Utica Jubilee Singers • Utica
  CONTEMPORARY STATUS
    Canton Spirituals • Canton
    Mississippi Mass Choir / Frank Williams • Jackson

JAZZ
  PIONEER STATUS
    Herbie Holmes • Yazoo City
    Jimmie Lunceford • Fulton
    Lester Young • Woodville
  CONTEMPORARY STATUS
    Mose Allison • Tippo
    Milt Hinton • Vicksburg
    Cassandra Wilson • Jackson

MOVIES AND TELEVISION
  CONTEMPORARY STATUS
    Dee Barton • Houston
    Mundell Lowe • Laurel

MUSICAL THEATER, BROADWAY
  PIONEER STATUS
    Lehman Engel • Jackson
  CONTEMPORARY STATUS
    Vicki Helms Carter • Tupelo
    Lloyd Wells • Laurel

POPULAR
  CONTEMPORARY STATUS
    Guy Hovis • Tupelo
    Nanette Workman • Jackson

Dr. Charles Elliott (right) presents LLoyd Wells with his Mississippi Musicians Hall of Fame award.

PRODUCTION, RECORDING AND PROMOTION
  PIONEER STATUS
    Jimmie Ammons / Delta Records Jackson
    Willard and Lillian McMurray / Diamond Records and Trumpet label • Jackson
    H.C. Speir • Jackson
    Johnny Vincent • Laurel
  CONTEMPORARY STATUS
    Malaco Records • Jackson
    Peavey Electronics Corp. • Meridian
    Rooster Blues Records • Clarksdale

RHYTHM AND BLUES, SOUL
  PIONEER STATUS
    Bo Diddley • McComb
    John Lee Hooker • Clarksdale
    Eddie "Guitar Slim" Jones Hollandale
  CONTEMPORARY STATUS
    Sam Cooke • Clarksdale
    Dorothy Moore • Jackson

ROCK AND ROLL
  PIONEER STATUS
    Bo Diddley • McComb
    Elvis Presley • Tupelo
    Ike Turner • Clarksdale
  CONTEMPORARY STATUS
    Jimmy Buffett • Pascagoula
    Jerry Lee Lewis • Nesbit, since 1973

SPECIAL
  Skeets McWilliams • Jackson

Blues

•••••

The word "blues" is associated with the ideas of depression, hard times, and sadness. Washington Irving, the American writer, coined the term in his writings around 1807.

   A mix of African and European music came about to form this uniquely American music. In an oppressive system, it was the Mississippi Delta black field hand, called the "holler," that gave rise to the blues. The blues expressed the suffering and extreme hardships of blacks in the South. By 1900 to 1920, the blues was sung in many rural areas of the South.

   European land owners taught blacks hymns and furnished them old world instruments to play. Blacks transformed these resources into their own musical expressions.

   Early blues performers relied on voice and acoustic guitar. Later, a microphone on a stand was added for the singer as he strummed the guitar. Still later, urban blues incorporated the electric guitar, harmonica, drums, and horns.

   Today, this uniquely Mississippi product is heard all over the world. It is at the roots of jazz, rhythm and blues, rock and roll, and popular music. It is part of America's music.

   This listing of blues artists is limited and is but a sample of these great artists. More than 300 noted blues musicians from Mississippi have been identified. Just over sixty are cited in this book.

Garfield Akers was born around 1900 near Brights and later moved to Hernando. He was playing the guitar as a teenager. The Akers family worked as typical Southern sharecroppers most of Akers' early life.

He met another blues guitarist from Hernando, Joe Callicott, around 1920, and they performed together until the 1940s. He and Callicott played parties and dances on weekends in the Delta.

The two recorded in the fall of 1929 for Vocalion/Brunswick in Memphis, and Akers and Callicott are reported to have made several recordings at that time. They backed each other with two sides written by Akers, *Dough Roller Blues* and *Jumpin' and Shoutin' Blues*. Akers is said to have developed the "stompin' bass" that was featured on his recording of *Cottonfield Blues*.

Akers died in Memphis in 1958.

Roosevelt "Booba" Barnes was born September 25, 1936, on a plantation in Longwood. He started playing the harmonica when he was seven. His name "Booba" came from a brother who described him as a booby trap. Like so many other young blues musicians, he earned a little money playing in front of stores and at parties.

He began to play the guitar in his late teens. At seventeen, his first real work came in Rolling Fork with the Swinging Gold Coasters. They played in the Mississippi Delta and nearby Arkansas. Barnes did some recording as backup harmonica in Chicago and played clubs in Gary, Indiana. He eventually returned to Mississippi and opened a club in Greenville. He recorded two songs, *How Many More Years Must This Go On* and *Heartbroken Man*. He died in Chicago of lung cancer in 1996 at the age of 59.

Eddie Riley "Little Eddie" Boyd was born Edward Riley Boyd in Stovall on November 25, 1914, and moved to Chicago in 1941. He was one of the most popular piano-playing bluesmen around Chicago in the early 1950s. His *Five Long Years* is a blues classic. Other of his recordings include *Ain't Doin' Too Bad, All the Way, Come on Home, Eddie's Blues, I'm Going Home,* and many more.

Eddie died in Helsinki, Finland, where he had lived with his Finnish wife.

Ishmon Bracey was born in Byram on January 9, 1901. He was one of the early giants of the blues. Bracey made his first recordings in Memphis in 1928 for the Victor label. Two years later he traveled to Grafton, Wisconsin, to record for Paramount. He all but abandoned his blues roots when he became an ordained minister sometime in the late 1940s or early 1950s. Bracey continued to play music, but it was mostly religious standards. He spent most of his years preaching in the Hinds County area. He died in Jackson on February 12, 1970.

Jackie Brenson was born in Clarksdale on August 15, 1930. He had a No. 1 hit record in 1951, *Rocket 88,* considered by many to be the first true rock and roll record. The song was written by two other Mississippians, Ike Turner (who played with Brenson on the record) and Delta bluesman James Cotton.

Other of his recordings include *Real Gone Rocket, Hi-Ho Baby,* and *Tuckered Out.* He also played saxophone with Ike Turner's King of Rhythm in 1956. Brenson died in Memphis on December 15, 1979.

William Lee Conley "Big Bill" Broonzy was born in Scott (Bolivar County) on June 26, 1893. He moved to rural Arkansas at an early age where he played a homemade violin.

As a young man, he worked on his farm and served in World War I before moving to Chicago and learning to play the guitar. In the 1920s he began a long recording career.

Broonzy was one of the better known blues players and recorded more than 260 blues songs including *Feelin' Low Down, Remember Big Bill, Make Me Getaway,* and *Big Bill Broonzy Sings Country Blues.*

He died in Chicago on August 15, 1958.

"Howlin' Wolf" Burnett was born Chester Arthur Burnett in White Station in Clay County on June 10, 1910. Burnett was six-foot-six and weighed close to 300 pounds in his

> **Mississippi First:**
> "HOWLIN' WOLF" BURNETT, BORN IN CLAY COUNTY, FIRST DEVELOPED AND FOUNDED THE CHICAGO ELECTRIC BLUES.

prime and had a raspy, sandpaper growl of a voice. He did not start recording until the 1950s, first at Sun Records in Memphis and then Chess in Chicago.

He was known as the founder of the Chicago electric blues which is an urban rendition of the Delta blues. He recorded such blues classics as *How Many More Years, Riding in the Moonlight, Spoonful, Willie Ain't Superstitious,* and *Back Door Man.* Although relatively unknown for many years in the United States, Burnett was hugely popular in England. He recorded a prodigious total of 67 albums during his career. He recorded for Chess, MCA, Charly, Vogue, New Rose, and Sound Solutions.

He was inducted into the Rock & Roll Hall of Fame in 1991 in the Early Influences category. On September 17, 1994, the U.S. Postal Service issued postage stamps commemorating eight Legends of Blues and Jazz. Burnett was one of three Mississippians honored on those stamps (the other two were Robert Johnson and Muddy Waters). He died in Hines, Illinois, on January 10, 1976.

R. L. Burnside was born November 23, 1926, near Oxford. He grew up with blues artists like Fred McDowell and Muddy Waters, who married Burnside's aunt. After watching and listening to them play, Burnside tried his luck playing the guitar. He played with simple three-note riffs and single chord stroking.

He has since been playing the blues for forty years. However, he was not "discovered" until around 1990. He has recorded on Sony and Columbia.

He has made more than five albums and played shows like the Spencer Blues Explosion. Some of his albums include *Mississippi Delta Blues, Hill Country Blues, Mississippi Blues, Sound Machine Groove,* and *Too Bad Jim.*

Burnside has developed a blues cult following that likes his raw, energetic trance music. His latest album, though, *Come On In,* is off that style.

Burnside has been called one of the last purists of the real Mississippi blues. He made a video recording of *Rollin' Tumblin',* which has been played on MTV.

"Bo" Carter was born Armenter Chatmon in Bolton on March 21, 1893. He was the brother of Mississippi bluesmen Sam and Lonnie Chatmon. He made more than one hundred recordings of mostly "hokum" blues, Delta blues with sexy lyrics. Some of his best-known songs are *Sue Cow, Who's Been Here, Pussy Cat Blues,* and *Banana In Your Fruit Basket.*

He worked with Charlie McCoy and Texas Alexander; and his songs were used by Count Basie, Jerry Lee Lewis, and Merle Haggard. He was influenced by John Hurt and Big Bill Broonzy. Chatmon's influence can be heard on early Bob Dylan records. He died in Memphis on September 21, 1964.

Sam Chatmon was born in Bolton on January 10, 1897, and was the brother of Bo Carter (Armenter Chatmon) and Lonnie Chatmon, who led the famous Mississippi Sheiks. The Chatmon family was well-known in Mississippi for its broad musical talents. The Chatmon family string band, of which Sam was sometimes a member in his youth, regularly performed for white audiences in the early 1900s.

He continued Bo's tradition of double-meaning-lyrics blues but also showed a serious side in the early anthology *I Have To Paint My Face.*

In addition to playing first generation blues, the Chatmon band also played ragtime, ballads, and popular dance tunes. Like other bluesmen of the day, Sam per-

Sam Chatmon

BLUES • 16

formed at parties and on street corners throughout much of Mississippi for small pay and tips.

In the 1930s, he recorded with the Mississippi Sheiks and the Chatmon Brothers. Sam Chatmon settled down in Hollandale, Mississippi, in the early 1940s and worked on area plantations. He was "rediscovered" in 1960 and began his new career as a folk-blues artist. In 1960, Sam recorded for the Arhoolie label, which led to other labels in the 1960s and 1970s. Some of his songs include *Ash Tray Taxi, Go Back Old Devil, She's My Baby,* and *Winter Time Blues.*

He also toured extensively during these two decades, capitalizing on the blues revival that had swept through folk circles. He played many of the largest and best-known folk festivals, including the Smithsonian Festival of American Folklife in Washington, D.C., in 1972; the Mariposa Festival in Toronto in 1974; and the New Orleans Jazz & Heritage Festival in 1976. Chatmon continued to record and perform until his death in Hollandale on February 2, 1984.

Eddy "The Chief" Clearwater, whose real name was Eddie Harrington, was born January 10, 1935, in Macon. He would later be known as Eddy Clearwater, a takeoff on Muddy Waters' name. However, his first stage name was "Guitar Eddy." When Clearwater was thirteen, his family moved to Birmingham, Alabama where began backing various gospel groups on his guitar including the legendary Five Blind Boys.

Eddy "The Chief" Clearwater

At age fifteen, still playing gospel music, Clearwater traveled to Chicago's West Side in September 1950.

Clearwater worked as a cab driver during the day. He played local Chicago nightclubs for decades and also recorded singles for labels like Atomic-H, LaSalle, and Federal. Clearwater combines 1950s rock and roll, gospel, soul, country, and blues into his own unique sound. He plays his guitar with his left hand and upside down.

In 1961, he recorded *I Was Gone, A Real Good Time,* and *Twist Like This* for Federal Records.

He toured Europe twice in the late 1970s, made appearances on England's BBC television, and recorded for France's MCM Company. The first release on

Rooster Blues label was Clearwater's 1980 United States debut album, *The Chief.* Rooster Blues Records was a Mississippi label at that time, located in Clarksdale.

Clearwater's next album was recorded for England's Red Lightnin' label and won a W. C. Handy Award for "Best Import Blues Album." Two more albums for Rooster Blues followed: *Flimdoozie* (1986) and *A Real Good Time … Live!* (1990). Other albums include *Blues Hangout,* and *Help Yourself* in 1992.

A successful session with Ralph Bass from 1977 was released as *Boogie My Blues* on Delmark in 1995. Clearwater's first album for Bullseye Blues and Jazz, *Mean Case of the Blues,* was issued in 1997. *Don't Take My Blues,* a song from *Mean Case of the Blues* won a 1998 W. C. Handy Award nomination for "Blues Song for the Year."

Clearwater was nominated for the W. C. Handy Award as "Artist Most Deserving of Wider Recognition." Clearwater's 1998 Bullseye Blues and Jazz releases was *Cool Blues Walk. Chicago Daily Blues* and *Reservation Blues* followed in mid-2000.

Clearwater tours the United States, Canada, Europe, Asia, and South America.

James Cotton was born in Tunica, Mississippi, on July 1, 1935. He co-wrote, with Ike Turner, what was probably the first rock and roll hit, *Rocket 88.* Eighteen of his albums are available.

His first LP was *The James Cotton Band* but his classic LP was *100% Cotton.* His songs include *Boogie Thing, How Long Can a Fool Go Wrong,* and *The Creeper Creeps Again.*

Arthur William "Big Boy" Crudup was born in Forest on August 24, 1905 and was said to be a big influence on Elvis. He wrote *That's All Right Mama,* the first song Presley released.

Crudup began his musical career singing gospel in church choir, and started playing the blues for parties in Clarksdale in 1939.

In 1940, Crudup moved to Chicago hoping to make a better living as a musician. For a while, he played blues on street corners in Chicago. Finally, he was discovered by blues producer Lester Melrose. Crudup was hired to play at a party at producer Tampa Red's house in 1941. As a result, he was signed to record for RCA/Bluebird. He continued to record with RCA in the late 1940s and 1950s, and toured with Sonny Boy Williamson and Elmore James.

He played the guitar and harmonica, sang, and wrote other blues classics which were used by famous artists such as B. B. King, Big Mama Thornton, Bobby "Blue" Bland, and Elvis Presley. Three of Crudup's songs were recorded by Elvis.

By the mid 1950s Crudup had all but quit the music business because he was angry at being cheated out of money.

He returned to Mississippi after a disagreement with Melrose and ran a successful bootlegging business.

Later, he made a comeback with an album for Bobby Robinson and recorded on Delmark and Liberty labels. He toured England in 1969, Australia in 1972, and played in blues revival concerts like the Newport Jazz Festival. A film documentary of his life was made in 1973.

Crudup will be remembered as a great bluesman and songwriter. He died in Nassawadox, Virginia, on March 28, 1974.

Mississippi First:

THE U.S. POSTAL SERVICE PUBLISHED EIGHT STAMPS ENTITLED "LEGENDS OF BLUES AND JAZZ." MISSISSIPPIANS WERE FIRST IN NUMBER ON THAT LIST OVER ANY OTHER STATE, WITH THREE LEGENDARY BLUES MUSICIANS FEATURED— "HOWLIN' WOLF" BURNETT, ROBERT JOHNSON, AND MUDDY WATERS.

"Blind" John Davis was born in Hattiesburg on December 7, 1913. His blues piano was featured on dozens of blues records during the 1930s and 1940s. He accompanied artists such as Sonny Boy Williamson, Tampa Red, and Big Bill Broonzy. He was the first pianist to do a European blues tour (with Broonzy in 1952). Four of his albums are available and include *Stompin' on a Saturday Night* in 1978, *You Better Cut That Out* in 1985, and *Blind John Davis* in 1995. He died in Chicago on October 12, 1985.

"Big" Willie James Dixon was born in Vicksburg on July 1, 1915. Born the seventh of fourteen children, Dixon was greatly influenced by his mother, Daisy, who turned everything she said into rhymes.

However, his first real musical influence came at the age of seven. He often left school to hear a band starring pianist Little Brother Montgomery. As a youth, Dixon sang with the Union Jubilee singers, a gospel quartet with its own radio program.

After a short career in boxing, he began his musical career by forming the Five Breezes in 1940 with Leonard "Baby Doo" Caston. They recorded blues songs until 1941. Dixon formed a new group, the Four Jumps of Jive, that later recorded for Mercury.

In 1945, Caston and Dixon teamed up to form the Big Three Trio along with guitarist Benardo Dennis and landed a recording contract first with Bullet Records and, in 1947, with Columbia Records. Dixon eventually went to work at Chess Records because of his ability to read, write, compose, and arrange music, which made him the mainstay of Chess. Dixon was also considered the main leader of the Chess Records operation.

Throughout the 1970s, Dixon released albums on the Ovation, Columbia, and Yamboo labels. In 1980, Dixon was inducted into the Blues Foundation's Hall of Fame, and in 1982 Dixon established the Blues Heaven Foundation to help musicians and their estates claim royalty payments.

In 1988, he released *Hidden Charms* with Bug/Capitol; and in 1989, Dixon published his autobiography, *I Am the Blues,* coauthored by Don Snowden. He appeared in the films *Raw Justice* (1994), *Good Cop, Bad Cop* (1994), *Night of the Warrior* (1991), and *Rich Girl* (1990). He also wrote original music for the movie *Ginger Ale Afternoon* (1989).

Dixon's songs were recorded by such musicians as Muddy Waters, Howlin' Wolf, Elvis Presley, The Rolling Stones, the Grateful Dead, and the Doors. The most noted were *I Just Want to Make Love to You* for Waters and *I'm Ready* for Wolf. Dixon died at the age of seventy-six at St. Joseph's Medical Center in Burbank, California, on January 29, 1992.

K. C. Douglas was born in Sharon on November 21, 1913. He moved to California in 1945 where he continued his down home guitar and vocal style. His first album was titled *K. C. Douglas, A Dead Beat Guitar and the Mississippi Blues.* His own composition, *Mercury Boogie,* was recorded by the Steve Miller Band. Six of his albums are available and include *Road Recording, Big Road Blues, K. C.'s Blues,* and *Mercury Boogie.* He died in Berkeley, California, on October 18, 1975.

David "Honeyboy" Edwards was born in Shaw on June 28, 1915. There

Honeyboy Edwards

he taught himself how to play the guitar by listening to area bluesmen like Tommy McClennan and Robert Petway.

By age fourteen, he was playing Delta juke joints and picnics with Big Joe Williams. During the 1930s and 1940s, he played with people like McClennan, Robert Johnson, Big Walter Horton, and Yank Rachell. A boyhood friend of blues legend Robert Johnson, he often played guitar with him at juke joints.

Edwards played traditional and old style Mississippi Delta blues after he left his home in Shaw for Chicago at the age of fourteen. *The New York Times* calls Edwards one of "the last authentic performers in blues idiom that developed in central Mississippi during the second and third decades of the century."

Blues historian Alan Lomax recorded Edwards for the Library of Congress in 1942. Edwards didn't record professionally until he got to Houston, Texas in 1951 and recorded *Who May Your Regular Be* for Arc Records. He had a hit song, *Drop Down Mama* in 1953.

He played small clubs and on street corners in Chicago with Johnnie Temple, Floyd Jones, and Kansas City Red. In the mid-1960s, he resumed his recording career with the Adelphi/Blue Horizon label and began to play festivals.

He toured Europe and Japan mainly during the 1970s and 1980s and performed at the Smithsonian's Festival of American Folklife, the Chicago Blues Festival, and the San Francisco Blues Festival.

In 1992, his album *Delta Bluesman* was released. This work includes Edwards' original Library of Congress recordings and his songs of that time. In 1998, he published his autobiography, *The World Don't Owe Me Nothin'* and had an album by the same name.

Lillian "Lil" Green was born in the Delta on December 22, 1919. She learned blues singing in church and country juke joints. She went to Chicago in the 1930s and performed with some of Mississippi's finest blues figures, including Big Bill Broonzy. They worked the "chitlin' circuit," back yard parties, together. Green recorded Broonzy's *Country Boy Blues*. Her composition, *Romance In the Dark,* was a 1940 Bluebird hit; and in 1941, she followed it with *Why Don't You Do Right?* later sung by Peggy Lee. She died in Chicago on April 14, 1954.

Earl Zebebee Hooker was born in Clarksdale on January 15, 1930. Generally acknowledged by his peers as the finest all-around guitarist in Chicago blues circles, his slide guitar work was the most technically advanced of all bluesmen. His songs include *Bertha, Blue Guitar, Hot and Heavy, Moon Is Rising, Off the Hook,* and *Two Bugs and a Roach.* Hooker recorded eighteen albums and was a sideman on numerous sessions. He was the cousin of John Lee Hooker. He died in Chicago on April 21, 1970.

> •••••
> ## Mississippi First:
> MISSISSIPPI IS THE BIRTHPLACE OF THE BLUES, THE FIRST OF AMERICA'S DISTINCT MUSIC TYPES.
> •••••

John Lee Hooker was born in Clarksdale, on August 17, 1920. Delta blues legend Charlie Patton was his childhood inspiration.

Hooker worked as a janitor in a Detroit auto factory by day and played the blues by night. He signed a record contract in Detroit with Riverside Records in 1948 and had a million sales

John Lee Hooker

for his *Boogie Chillen.*

He was a blues-stylist who had a major influence on R&B and rock and roll. Johnny Rivers recorded some of his songs; and his hit *Boom Boom* was played by The Animals. An album, *Chill Out,* was released February 1995; and he was inducted into the Rock & Roll Hall of Fame in 1991.

In 1998, at age 81, he had a number of achievements, including a Grammy and a lifetime achievement award from the Rhythm and Blues Foundation.

Some experts think English groups like the Yardbirds, discovered Hooker in the 1960s.

Walter "Shakey" Horton was born at Horn Lake on April 6, 1917. With nicknames "Shakey" and "Big Walter," he recorded with a Memphis jug band before moving to Chicago. He was one of the all-time great blues harmonica players and helped define modern-amplified harps. He played backup harmonica for Muddy Waters and bluesman Jimmy Rogers.

Seven of his albums are available. His most notable include *Big Walter's Boogie, Easy, Jumpin' Blues, They Call Me Big Walter,* and *Walter's Blues.* He died in Chicago on December 8, 1981.

Eddie James "Son" House was born in Riverton on March 21, 1902, the second of three brothers. When he was about seven, his parents separated; and his mother took the boys south to Tallulah, Louisiana.

At age of fifteen, he started preaching near Lyon, Mississippi, and did not start playing the guitar until he was about twenty-six. House met Charlie Patton in 1929 and went to Wisconsin to record "race" records for Paramount.

He moved to New York state in 1940 and came home to Mississippi to visit in 1942. At that time, Alan Lomax recorded House for the Library of Congress.

As a result of that "discovery," he made many successful appearances. He was the last great voice of the first generation of bluesmen and a tremendous influence on Robert Johnson, Muddy Waters, and many others. A teenage Robert Johnson heard Son House play and as a result, abandoned the harmonica for the guitar.

He started to get recognition by playing with Charlie Patton, Willie Brown, and other well-known jazz musicians. He even played for a while with Robert Johnson. He recorded some of his most famous works in 1929: *My Black Mama* and *Preachin' the Blues* for Alan Lomax. House was, however, always torn between the sacred and the blues.

Son House

House retired as a musician in 1960, but in 1964 he came out of retirement to sign with Columbia Records. He then recorded and performed from 1964 to 1976. In 1969, House made a short film called *Son House* and was inducted into the Blues Foundation Hall of Fame in 1980.

Columbia released *Father of the Delta Blues* in 1992, a boxed set of his songs.

He died on his eighty-sixth birthday in Detroit on March 21, 1988.

"Mississippi" John Smith Hurt was born at Teoc on, July 1, 1892, and moved to Avalon at age two.

Hurt played an old style guitar not associated with the bluesmen of that time. He first recorded in 1928 and recorded eighteen albums of gentle, finger-picked blues. His most noted single selections include *Candy Man, Avalon Blues, Spike Driver Blues,* and *Stagger Lee Blues,* all recorded for OKeh Records. Hurt enjoyed a second musical career when he was "rediscovered" in 1963, even appearing on "The Tonight Show" with Johnny Carson. He died in Grenada on November 2, 1966.

Vasti Jackson was born on October 20, 1959, in McComb. He learned to play guitar from his maternal grandfather and grandmother. From a young age, he played the blues from local juke joints to major stages in America, Europe, South America, and Scandinavia. Vasti has performed at the Monterey Jazz Festival, New Orleans Jazz and Heritage Festival, Chicago Blues Festival, Jubilee Jam, Saint Louis Blues Festival, and the Delta Blues Festival.

He has composed, performed, and produced music for the Discovery Channel, HBO, VH1, BBC (England), City TV (Canada), the "Good Day Show" (Australia), XFM Radio (Uruguay), Global TV (Brazil), Norwegian National Television, Cox Cable, WGN, and A&E. He also served as musical director for the acclaimed national television show, "Blues Goin' On."

He recorded with the King of the Blues, B. B. King, on his Grammy Award winning *Blues Summit* release and also worked with Pulitzer Prize winner Wynton Marsalis on Warner Brothers' movie *Rosewood* soundtrack.

He worked with Z. Z. Hill, Johnnie Taylor, and Katie Webster. As a guitarist,

Vasti Jackson

he performed and/or recorded with blues legends Bobby Bland, Denise LaSalle, Little Milton, and Bobby Rush. In the tradition of Zydeco, he co-produced albums with legendary artist C. J. Chenier; and in the gospel arena, he performed and recorded with Phillip Bailey of Earth, Wind and Fire, gospel greats like The Williams Brothers, The Jackson Southernaires, and Daryl Coley.

Jackson worked as musical director for the film *Stop Breakin' Down,* the story of the life of Robert Johnson. He composed two songs for the soundtrack. His work has been featured in magazines like *Guitar Player, Living Blues, Nothing But the Blues, Juke Blues,* and many other international publications.

International tours have taken Jackson to Japan, Germany, France, Netherlands, Sweden, Switzerland, Italy, Sardinia, Norway, Finland, Argentina, Canada, Australia, England, Uruguay, Brazil, and Portugal. He was also recorded live for the Library of Congress' Local Legacy Series that will be on display at the library's Folk Life archives.

He now lives in Hattiesburg where he continues to record and tour.

Elmore James was born at Richland in Holmes County on January 27, 1918. By age ten, he was playing a self-made guitar and singing the blues. He is said to have introduced the electric guitar to the Delta in 1945 and helped define the modern electric Chicago blues sound of today. In 1951, he recorded for Lillian McMurray's Trumpet Records in Jackson. Heavily influenced by Robert Johnson, James became well-known after recording his own version of Johnson's *I Believe I'll Dust My Broom.* In fact, he named his band the Broom Dusters.

He traveled throughout the Delta playing intense, emotional blues that pleased audiences. He was a great slide guitarist who influenced many modern blues guitarists including Duane Allman, Jimi Hendrix, Johnny Winter, Eric Clapton, and others. He recorded fifty-eight albums that contained songs such as *Standing at the Crossroads, The Sky Is*

Crying, Look Over Yonder Wall, and *Something Inside of Me.*

He was inducted into the Rock and Roll Hall of Fame in 1992 in the "Early Influences" category. He died of a heart attack on May 24, 1963, and was buried near Durant, Mississippi.

"Skip" James was born Nehemiah Curtis James in Bentonia on June 9, 1902.

James played the piano and organ in the local Baptist church and learned to play the guitar in the John Hurt style. He developed a three-finger picking style on his own.

In 1931, he went to Wisconsin. There he recorded twenty-six sides of his own compositions. His *20-20* was composed on the spot. He toured with a gospel quartet that was organized by his father in 1931, and he later became an ordained Baptist minister.

He was one of the earliest and most influential Delta bluesmen. Robert Johnson recorded James' *Devil Got My Woman* retitled as *Hellhound On My Trail*. Eric Clapton recorded James' *I'm So Glad* on the first Cream album. James recorded a total of twelve albums during his career. His albums include *She Lyin'* by Genes in 1964, *Skip James Today!* by Vanguard in 1965, *I'm So Glad* by Vanguard in 1978, and *Blues From the Delta* by Vanguard in 1998. He died in Philadelphia on October 3, 1969.

Luther "Guitar Junior" Johnson was born in Itta Bena on April 11, 1939. Luther was named after his father, a sharecropper. He and his four sisters grew up on a farm named Forty Miles Bend, so called because the farm was forty miles in every direction.

Johnson, interested in music at an early age, got his first guitar from his mother when he was eleven and taught himself how to play. At the age of thirteen, Johnson led the church choir and formed his first gospel group at about age fourteen. In 1955, Johnson moved to Chicago where his sister got him a job at Scotty and Daralene's Rock 'N' Roll Inn.

In 1972, Johnson joined the Muddy Waters Band and in 1980 he started his own band called Magic Rockers. In 1982, Johnson moved to Boston, Massachusetts, where he developed a popular blues act. Johnson has recorded several CDs including *Ma Bea's Rock,*

Skip James

Robert Johnson

Luther's Blues, I Want to Groove with You, and *Doin' the Sugar Too.* Johnson won several Grammy Nominations and in 1984, he won a Grammy Award for his *Walkin' The Dog.*

> **Mississippi First:**
> ROBERT JOHNSON, FROM HAZLEHURST, IS LISTED AS FIRST IN INFLUENCING THE BLUES.

Robert Johnson was born on May 8, 1911, in Hazlehurst and grew up near Robinsonville. Through Willie Brown, Son House and Charlie Patton, Johnson became intimately familiar with Delta blues styles. After extensive study with the unrecorded Ike Zinermon in the early 1930s, Johnson emerged an inventive and rhythmic guitarist with phenomenal technique, especially in regard to his slide guitar method, and a gifted and emotional singer.

Johnson brought about the full flowering of the Mississippi Delta blues through his late-1930s recordings of only twenty-nine songs, but they're among the greatest in the genre, including *Terraplane Blues, I Believe I'll Dust My Broom, Ramblin' On My Mind, Cross Road Blues, Walkin' Blues, Love In Vain Blues, Stop Breakin' Down Blues,* and *Sweet Home Chicago.* The 1961 reissue of his finest work, entitled *King of the Delta Blues Singers,* forever altered the direction of popular music by providing musical cornerstones for contemporary blues musicians Eric Clapton, The Rolling Stones, Led Zeppelin, and countless others and established him as the watershed artist who bridged the Mississippi Delta blues, electric Chicago blues, and rock and roll.

His influence on popular music culture, and, in turn, its obsession with all things Johnson is chronicled in Robert Mugge's excellent 1999 documentary film, *Hellhounds On My Trail—The Afterlife of Robert Johnson.* By any account, Robert Johnson is among the most influential of all musical artists of the 20th century.

Johnson was inducted into the Rock and Roll Hall of Fame in 1986 as an "Early Influence." His *Complete Recordings,* a 2-CD boxed set issued in 1990, spent seven months on *Billboard's* Top Pop Albums chart, outselling twenty times over every other album of its kind ever issued and earning Grammy awards for its producers in 1991.

It's said that Johnson sold his soul to the devil in exchange for his ability to play and sing the blues better than any other man. That myth is central to the 1986 movie *Crossroads,* which was filmed on location in the Delta towns of Beulah, Bolivar, Chatham, Greenville, Murphy, Vicksburg, and Winterville. The factual story of his life and music, however, is brilliantly depicted in *Can't You Hear The Wind Howl?,* the 1998 docu-drama narrated by Danny Glover.

It's also said that his untimely death on

August 16, 1938, was at the hands of a jealous husband who poisoned his drink at the Three Forks juke joint outside Greenwood.

On September 17, 1994, the United States Postal Service issued postage stamps commemorating eight "Legends of Blues and Jazz." Robert Johnson was one of three Mississippians so honored. (The others were Howlin' Wolf and Muddy Waters.)

Robert Johnson has become the international icon representing not only the Mississippi Delta blues, but all acoustic blues. He was recently inducted into the Mississippi Musicians Hall of Fame. In 1999, Robert Johnson received the prestigious Peavine Award and was inducted into the Mississippi Delta Blues Hall of Fame at Delta State University in Cleveland, Mississippi.

Tommy Johnson was born in Terry in 1896. He was one of the great blues musicians of the late 1920s and early 1930s. He was influenced by Charlie Patton. He, in turn, influenced artists like Howlin' Wolf and Floyd Jones. His best known works, vocal and guitar, are *Cool Drink of Water Blues* and *Canned Heat Blues*. He was inducted into the Blues Foundation's Hall of Fame in 1987. He died in Crystal Springs, November 1, 1956.

"Little" Johnny Jones was born in Jackson on November 1, 1924. He was one of the great blues pianists of all time and also played harmonica. He did very little solo recording but cut some sides with slide guitarist legend Elmore James. What few recordings of his work exist are considered classics of the Chicago style. Alligator Records did release *Live in Chicago With Billy Roy Arnold* in 1979 which captures Jones' vocal and piano style.

He died in Chicago on November 19, 1964.

Junior Kimbrough was born on July 28, 1930, and raised in Hudsonville where he learned how to play guitar by listening to records of Delta bluesmen. In 1968, he recorded his first single, *Tramp*, for the local Philwood label.

For the next two decades, Kimbrough didn't have the opportunity to record, but he played in juke joints throughout Mississippi, which is where music journalist Robert Palmer discovered him in the late 1980s.

Palmer featured Kimbrough in his documentary film *Deep Blues*. The exposure in the movie helped him get a national record contract. He signed with Fat Possum and released his first full-length album, *All Night Long,* in 1992. The record was given good reviews by both blues and mainstream publications, as was *Deep Blues* and its accompanying soundtrack. All of this success led to performances outside of the Delta, including tours in England. After 1992, Kimbrough returned to playing juke joints in the Delta. He recorded occasionally and released his second album, *Sad Days, Lonely Nights*, in 1993, *Haven't*

B. B. King with his famous guitar, Lucille.

Worked Out in 1997, and *God Knows I Tried* a year later.

Kimbrough died on January 17, 1998, of a heart attack.

B. B. King was born Riley B. King at Itta Bena on September 16, 1925. King was musically influenced by a preacher named Archie Fair at the Holiness Church in Carmichael. He taught King how to play guitar and sing early in life.

In 1947 with his guitar and $2.50, he hitchhiked north to Memphis, Tennessee, to follow his musical career. The first big break came for King in 1948 when he performed on Sonny Boy Williamson's radio program on KWEM out of West Memphis. This appearance led to steady performances for King.

About this same time he became a full-time disc jockey. His stage name started when he was called, "the Beale Street Blues Boy," which was shortened to "Blues Boy," then to "B. B."

Since King started recording in the late 1940s, he has released more than fifty albums. Many of these albums are considered blues classics.

His first record was *Miss Martha King* (1949), followed by *Three O'Clock Blues,* a major national R&B hit of the 1950s. He also had *Rock Me Baby, Woke Up This Morning, Paying the Cost to Be the Boss, Sweet Little Angel, Eyesight to the Blind, The Thrill Is Gone,* and many more.

During the 1970s, King toured Ghana, Lagos, Chad, and Liberia under the United States State Department. In 1989, King toured Australia, New Zealand, Japan, France, West Germany, Holland, and Ireland for three months as a special guest of the band U2.

He has called his guitar "Lucille" ever since nearly losing his life retrieving his guitar from a burning dance hall.

King also received numerous awards for achievements in various parts of music. Many prestigious colleges including Yale, Berkeley, and Rhodes College of Memphis gave King honorary doctorates.

He won the 1991 Grammy for Best Traditional Blues Album with his *Live at the Apollo,* and the 1994 Grammy in the same category with *Blues Summit.* He won the Grammy's Lifetime Achievement Award in 1987. He was inducted into the Rock and Roll Hall of Fame in 1986 and recently into the Mississippi Musicians Hall of Fame.

Denise LaSalle was born Denise Allen on July 16, 1939, in Leflore County and was raised in Belzoni across the street from a juke joint. She moved to Chicago in her early twenties and became a serious song writer. LaSalle recorded her first single, *A Love Reputation,* followed by one of her most memorable hits, *Married, But Not To Each Other.* She later signed with Westbound Records where she produced many of her biggest hits, including *Man Sized Job.*

LaSalle is also an accomplished songwriter. Her songs have been recorded by country greats like Barbara Mandrell and Rita Coolidge. LaSalle has written songs for Ann Peebles, Latimore, Little Milton, and Z. Z. Hill. She successfully recorded more than fourteen LPs during her musical career. Among her many achievements, she earned a Gold Record for her album, *Trapped By A Thing Called Love.* The record stayed at No. 1 on the R&B soul charts for sixteen weeks in 1971.

From 1976 to 1978, LaSalle recorded with ABC Records, which released her *Second Breath, The Bitch is Bad,* and *Under the Influence.* LaSalle then moved to MCA and released many hits including *Unwrapped.*

Her most popular hit was a fifteen minute remake of *Trapped by a Thing Called Love.* That number scored again in a medley with *Make Me Yours* and *Precious Precious.*

In 1982, LaSalle signed with Malaco Records in Jackson. Her first release was the hit *Lady In The Street.* Her second release on the Malaco label was *Right Place, Right Time* and featured Z. Z. Hill's *Down Home Blues.* LaSalle had enormous success with her third album, *Love Talkin',* which included the smash No. 1 hit *My Tu Tu.*

In 1996, Malaco released an album entitled *Denise*. LaSalle continues to perform and record for Malaco.

Albert "Sunnyland Slim" Luandrew was born in Vance on September 5, 1907. A strong, barrelhouse-style piano man, he has probably been on more recordings, both as sideman and leader, than any other blues pianist. His songs include *Anna Lou Blues, Broke and Hungry, Gotta See My Lawyer, Little Girl Blues, Mr. Cool,* and *Sunnyland Special.* Twenty-three of his albums are available.

"Magic Sam" or **"Good Rocking Sam" Maghett** was born Samuel Maghett outside Grenada on February 14, 1937. He taught himself to play on a homemade guitar at age ten. He drew on the church-based soul styling favored by fellow Mississippians B. B. King and Otis Rush.

He was the embodiment of 1960s Chicago blues at its best. He worked clubs and lounges in Chicago and toured Europe. He wrote many blues songs including *21 Days in Jail* and *Everything Gonna Be All Right.* Eighteen of his albums are available. He died December 1, 1969.

Tommy McClennan was born in Yazoo City on April 8, 1908. A gravel-throated blues singer, his 1939-42 Bluebird recordings include *Bottle It Up and Go, Cross Cut Saw Blues,* and *Deep Blue Sea Blues (Catfish Blues).* His albums include *Travelin' Highway Man, Bluebird Recording,* and *Guitar King.* McClennan died in Chicago in 1958.

Charlie McCoy was born in Jackson on May 26, 1909. Charlie was a blues singer and guitarist but also played the mandolin. His best work was recorded during the 1920s and 1930s. Twenty of his albums are available, with his *Complete Recorded Works (1928-1932)* released in 1992 by Document Records. He died in Chicago on July 26, 1950.

"Mississippi" Fred McDowell was born in Rossville, Tennessee, on January 12, 1904, but spent most of his life in Como, Mississippi. A driving bottleneck guitarist, he hoboed around the South during the 1920s and 1930s, spending a lot of time in Mississippi.

He was discovered and recorded by folklorist Alan Lomax in 1959. He was a major influence on Bonnie McDowell's *You Got To Move,* which was covered by *Rolling Stone* magazine. Some of his songs were *Annie Mae Blues, Black Minnie, Baby Let Me Lay Down, Eyes Like an Eagle,* and *Fred's Worried Life Blues.* He died in Memphis, Tennessee, on July 3, 1972.

"Little" Milton was born Milton Campbell, Jr., September 17, 1934, on a farm in the Mississippi Delta near Inverness. He was named after his father, Big Milton, who was a blues musician.

By working odd jobs, Little Milton earned enough to buy a guitar. In his

Little Milton

middle teenage years, he met Ike Turner and toured throughout the Mississippi Delta playing the blues.

Then in 1953, when Milton was eighteen, he got his first big break. It was in St. Louis at Bobbin Records where he wrote and recorded the songs, *I'm a Lonely Man* and *That Will Never Do,* that made Milton a recognized blues performer.

About 1960, Milton switched labels again and went with Checker Records. In 1965, he had a hit entitled *We're Gonna Make It.* Having a special meaning for blacks at the time, the song was his first big hit.

When the year 1971 came, Milton changed record labels again. This time he went with the Memphis-based Stax Record Company. Here he recorded a few more big hits including *Annie Mae's Cafe* and *Little Bluebird,* which became two of his most memorable songs. In 1984, he signed with Malaco Records in Jackson. While at Malaco, he wrote *The Blues Is Alright,* a song considered to be the blues anthem.

Milton has received numerous awards, including the W. C. Handy 1988 Blues Entertainer of the Year. He was also inducted into the Blues Hall of Fame that same year.

His album *I'm a Gambler,* released in 1996, has been a heavy seller. Milton has recorded more than twenty-six albums. Some of his latest from Malaco include *For Real* in 1998, *Welcome to Little Milton* in 1999, and *Reality* in 1999.

Mississippi Sheiks. This musical group, formed in Bolton, performed between 1930 and 1935, during which time they recorded more than eighty tracks for various "race" labels. (Race labels were considered to be for black performers.) The Mississippi Sheiks was a string band made up of members and friends of the Chatmon family, and included Lonnie Chatmon (guitar, violin), Sam Chatmon (guitar), Walter Vinson (guitar, violin), Bo Carter (Armenter Chatmon, guitar), and Charlie McCoy (banjo, mandolin). Singing chores were handled by all members. Most of these individuals pursued other musical careers from time to time. The instrumental abilities covered various musical styles from popular waltzes to party songs, with a fair amount of high-quality blues thrown in. Their work also appeared under names like Mississippi Mud Steppers, the Down South Boys, and The Carter Brothers. They recorded on the OKeh label.

(See also Bo Carter and Sam Chatmon)

"Muddy Waters" Morganfield was born McKinley Morganfield at Rolling Fork, on April 4, 1915. He was raised on the Stovall Plantation near Clarksdale where he began to sing, compose, and play the blues. Morganfield got his nickname as a child because he played near a muddy creek. Waters worked in a cotton field for fifty cents a day and there learned to sing while singing along with the other field hands.

At the age of seven, Morganfield learned to play the harmonica; and by seventeen he was playing the guitar. Morganfield received inspiration from blues greats like Son House and Robert Johnson.

He made numerous records for folklorist Alan Lomax, who collected songs for the Library of Congress. Two of Waters' songs, *I Be's Trouble* and *Country Blues*, were released on the Library of Congress anthology album. Morganfield made the two recordings before he left the plantation in Mississippi.

After moving to Chicago, he made recordings which included *Willie Can't Be Satisfied, Mean Red Spider, Sweet Lucy, Johnny Machine Gun,* and *Fly Right Little*

Muddy Waters, Father of Electric Blues.

Girl were released from 1946 to 1950. In the 1950s and 1960s, he had over a dozen hits including *She Moves Me, Caledonia, Baby Please Don't Go, Mannish Boy, Hoochie Coochie Man, Just Make Love to You, Rolling Stone,* and *Got My Mojo Workin'*.

Because his greatest records were released as singles, his first album, *The Best of Muddy Waters,* did not appear until 1958.

Morganfield's final two albums came in the early 1980s—*Muddy Mississippi*

> **Mississippi First:**
> "MUDDY WATERS" MORGANFIELD, BORN IN ROLLING FORK, WAS THE FIRST TO BE KNOWN AS "FATHER OF ELECTRIC BLUES."

Waters Live and *King Bee*. His most memorable performance came on the U.S. Tour at the White House when he played for President Jimmy Carter.

He won six Grammy awards and was inducted into the Rock and Roll Hall of Fame in 1986. On September 17, 1994, the U.S. Postal Service issued stamps commemorating "Legends of Blues and Jazz," including Muddy Waters and two other Mississippians, Howlin' Wolf and Robert Johnson. Muddy Waters has become known as the "Father of Electric Blues." Morganfield died in Westmont, Illinois on April 30, 1983.

Charles Douglas "Charlie" Musselwhite was born in Kosciusko on January 31, 1944. After high school, his family moved to Memphis, then to Chicago in the early 1960s. He learned to play the harmonica at age thirteen and frequently worked in family shows as a child.

In 1966, he appeared with Mike Bloomfield's Barry Goldberg Blues Band on WBBM-TV in Chicago. In 1967, he recorded his first album, *Stand Back Here Comes Charlie Musselwhite's South Side Blues Band*, on Vanguard. This release marked the beginning of his involvement in the "white blues movement." During 1971, Musselwhite recorded with John Lee Hooker on ABC/Dunhill label in San Francisco.

In 1974, Musselwhite performed at Stanford University in California and recorded on both Arhoolie and Capitol labels. However, his highest rated albums still include *Tennessee Woman* from Vanguard in 1969 and *Takin' My Time* from Arhoolie in 1974. He also made recordings in the 1980s and in the early 1990s for Alligator Records.

Sam Myers was born in Laurel on March 19, 1936. A solid blues harp player and singer, he contributed the solo on the Elmore James classic, *Look on Yonder Wall*. In 1957, Myers recorded a single, *My Love Is Here To Stay* and its flip side, *In the Ground* on the Ace label. He played harmonica with Anson and The Rockets where he was featured in concerts and on albums.

"Little Junior" Parker was born Herman Parker in Clarksdale, Mississippi, on March 27, 1932. He worked with Howlin' Wolf and B. B. King in the Memphis area and recorded *Mystery Train* on the Sun label, later a hit by Elvis Presley. He had a Top 10 R&B hit, *Driving Wheel*. He toured with Bobby "Blue" Bland and recorded twenty-three albums. He died on November 18, 1971.

Charlie Patton was born on May 1, 1887, in Hinds County near Edwards. When Patton was nine years old, his family moved to Dockery's plantation in the Mississippi Delta. He learned to play the guitar in his early teenage years and began playing blues.

It was on the plantation that Patton taught Son House and Willie Brown. Brown later used Patton's folk style on some of his recordings. Patton's lyrics described some of the themes of his life. He was tired of living a sharecropper's lifestyle. Patton also sang about the brutal and harsh conditions that African-Americans had in the South. The song, *Down the Dirt Road Blues,* tells the story of these conditions.

Patton never learned to read or write and became a traveling musician, making a minimal earning. He did not realize that his record contracts spelled his name Charley until later and asked that his name be spelled Charlie. He traveled along the Mississippi River, playing in different towns and began traveling to Georgia, Texas, Tennessee, Missouri, and Illinois.

His first record was *Pony Blues* which he was singing around 1921, but he had

Charlie Patton

been singing blues for more than ten years. One of his songs, *Mississippi Bo Weavil Blues,* was most likely taken from his experience with field hollers in the cotton fields.

Patton sang with a hoarse and loud tone. This style sometimes made it impossible to know the words he was singing. Some of the musicians that Patton influenced the most were Tommy Johnson, Bukka White, Big Joe Williams, Howlin' Wolf, and his regular partner, Willie Brown.

Patton made many recordings; but people seem to remember his early songs like *Hitch Up My Pony, Saddle Up My Grey Mare;* and *What You Want with a Rooster, He Won't Crow 'Fore Day?.*

> •••••
> ### Mississippi First:
> CHARLIE PATTON IS THE FIRST TO BE CALLED "KING OF THE DELTA BLUES."
> •••••

In 1933, Patton went to New York to record what were to be his last recordings. By then he was using a new clear style, and his performance on the records was good. Yet only four were released out of the fourteen he recorded. In Patton's short lifetime, he was married eight times. He was sometimes a difficult man to get along with, as he was an alcoholic and had problems controlling his temper.

He is known as the first great Delta bluesman, and his influence on those who followed is immense. In fact, he has been labeled the "King of the Delta Blues." Charlie Patton died of heart failure on April 28, 1934, at the age of forty-seven near Indianola on the Heathman-Dedham plantation.

> ### Mississippi First:
> "PINETOP" PERKINS, BORN IN BELZONI, WAS THE FIRST TO USE A STYLE OF BOOGIE-WOOGIE THAT FORMED THE BASIS FOR SWING AND ROCK AND ROLL.

Joe Willie "Pinetop" Perkins was born in Belzoni on July 13, 1913. He worked primarily as a guitarist during the 1930s and early 1940s. In the early years, he appeared with the King Biscuit Boys, Robert Nighthawk, and Earl Hooker. He also appeared with Sonny Boy Williamson.

Because of an arm injury, he switched to playing piano. Although Perkins never played swing, it was his brand of boogie-woogie that was shaped to form swing and eventually rock and roll. Boogie-woogie features a heavy walking base line.

He recorded *Pinetop's Boogie Woogie* for Sam Phillips in 1953. Perkins is perhaps best known for his work with Muddy Waters. He replaced Otis Spann (also from Belzoni) in the Muddy Waters Band in 1969. One of the world's top blues pianists, six of his albums are available. His own album, *After Hours*, on Blind Pig Records, was released in 1988.

Fenton Robinson was born in Minter City on September 23, 1935. He was a guitarist, singer, and composer. After recording Memphis style blues, he moved to Chicago in 1961 at age twenty-two.

He recorded his well-known popular hit, *Somebody Loan Me A Dime,* in 1967. In 1975, he signed with the Alligator label and began touring nationwide. His many Japanese fans have dubbed him "The Mellow Blues Genius." His jazz-flavored blues was well ahead of its time. In his later years, he taught the blues in Springfield, Illinois, and continued to perform on occasions.

He died in November 1997 in Rockford, Illinois.

Andy Rodgers, one of eighteen children, was born in Liberty on March 14, 1922, to sharecroppers Effie Sibley and Bailey Rodgers. He is part Cherokee. He worked the fields during the day and then would go to the night clubs to play harmonica and guitar. He bought his first guitar around 1930 from Bo Diddley.

He got his first harmonica at age ten. By age twelve, he was playing in a club where people would throw money at him. As a young teenager, Bob Wills and the Texas Playboys picked him up on the road; he traveled with them on tour and went to the Grand Ole Opry to play and record.

Rodgers played harmonica on Roy Acuff's radio station in the 1930s. Rodgers called himself the "Midnight Cowboy." Dustin Hoffman got the rights to use his name when he produced the movie, *Midnight Cowboy*. Rodgers eventually billed himself as the "Grand Daddy of the Blues."

Andy Rodgers, the Midnight Cowboy.

When Rodgers won "The Gong Show" twice in the 1970s, he got many calls to do shows and movies. You can hear his harmonica in the movie *The Big Easy*. Rodgers has been in commercials and TV interviews where he was seen in 1992 with Bill Cosby on his "You Bet Your Life" program. He was in the movie *Phenomenon* with John Travolta.

The Southern California Picture Council presented Rodgers with the Bronze Halo Award for outstanding contribution to the entertainment industry, along with Bo Jack Hollywood. In 1994, he received the Stars Award for actor and humanitarian in 1994. He got an award from the Black Cowboys Association in Oakland in 1994.

Rodgers has two released recordings; his first in 1993 was *Freight Train Blues* and in 1995, *Chicken Thief Blues*. Interviews can be found in *Living Blues* (1996), *American Harmonica* (Vol I, No 3, from Battlecreek, Michigan, 1997-98-99).

He was inducted into the Cowboy Blues Hall of Fame on September 25, 1998.

Rodgers says, "I don't feel dressed unless I have my cowboy wear on and I'm a naked and lonely boy without my harmonicas. I am Grand Daddy of the Blues; I been out here more than sixty years."

Jimmy Rogers (not the same as Jimmie Rodgers) was born James A. Lane in Ruleville on June 31, 1924. He played the guitar, harmonica, and piano and was a major figure in the development of postwar Chicago blues in the 1940s and 1950s.

Jimmy Rogers

He was best known for his Chess recordings: *That's All Right* (1950, a blues standard) and *Walking by Myself* (1956). He retained his own style with his Mississippi roots intact and is one of the few who never adapted the B. B. King and Albert King styles of string-bending.

Charles Isaiah "Doc" Ross was born in Tunica on October 21, 1925. He has an unusual guitar style in that he essentially plays the instrument backwards. He plays the guitar left-handed and upside-down and plays the harmonica turned around with the low notes to his right.

Early on, he recorded two classics on the Sun label in Memphis, *Chicago Breakdown* and *Boogie Disease*. He released six albums that include *Doctor Ross Rockin'*, *Going Back South*, *Mississippi Blues*, *Train Fare Home*, *Industrial Blues*, and *Juke Box Boogie*.

"Little" Otis Rush was born in Philadelphia, Mississippi, on April 29, 1934. As a child, Rush worked in the fields to help his mother. Rush, along with his other brothers and sisters, had to support themselves without help from a father.

Rush moved to Chicago in 1948 and by then had learned to play the guitar, which he played upside down and left-handed. He also learned to play the harmonica as a child in Mississippi.

Rush gained enough respect in Chicago blues circles to secure a recording contract with Cobra Records in 1956. His first release was a single, *Can't Quit You Baby*. It became number nine on the Top 10 chart.

For a time, he recorded with Chess Records, Duke Records, Atlantic Records, Capitol Records, and Quicksilver Recording Company.

His unique style influenced many young guitarists such as Jimmy Page, Eric Clapton, and Stevie Ray Vaughan. He recorded twenty albums, including *Ain't Enough Comin' In* (1994). Also a songwriter, his *She's A Good 'Un* was an early hit and *Homework* a big single in 1962.

In 1975, he won the International Critics Award for Soul-R&B from *Downbeat* magazine.

Otis Spann was born in Belzoni on March 21, 1930. After his discharge from the army in 1951, he moved to Chicago where he performed with Memphis Slim, Little Brother, and Roosevelt Sykes. He played piano in the band backing Muddy Waters who, Spann claimed, was his half-brother. He is considered the greatest blues piano player the Chicago blues scene has ever produced and recorded twenty-eight albums. He died in Chicago on April 24, 1970.

Hubert Sumlin was born in Greenwood on November 16, 1931. A longtime sideman with Howlin' Wolf, he did the great guitar work on all of Wolf's Chess singles of the late 1950s and early 1960s. Guitar great Jimi Hendrix once wrote, "My favorite guitar player is Hubert Sumlin." Seven of his albums are available including *My Guitar and Me, Groove, Blues Party, Heart and Soul,* and *Blues Anytime!*

Eddie "Playboy" Taylor was born at Benoit on January 29, 1923. He started as a juke-joint bluesman in Mississippi in the late 1930s. Some of his songs include *Bad Boy, I Feel So Bad, Playboy Boogie, 13 Highways,* and *You'll Always Have a Home.* He recorded seven albums and played the boogie lines on all of Jimmy Reed's hit records. Taylor died on Christmas Day, 1985, in Chicago.

"Hound Dog" Taylor was born Theodore Roosevelt Taylor in Natchez on April 12, 1917. A very influential slide guitarist, he was the first blues artist to record on Alligator Records in 1971. He helped launch Alligator Records with albums like *Natural Boogie, Hound Dog Taylor and The Houserockers,* and *Beware of the Dog.* He died in Chicago on December 17, 1975.

> •••••
> **Mississippi First:**
> JOHNNIE "GEECHIE" TEMPLE, BORN IN CANTON, WAS THE FIRST TO DEVELOP THE NOW-STANDARD BOTTOM STRING BOOGIE-WOOGIE BASS FIGURE.
> •••••

Johnnie "Geechie" Temple was born in Canton on October 18, 1906. He is one of the great unsung heroes of the blues. A contemporary of Son House, Skip James, and other Delta legends, he was the first to develop the now-standard bottom-string boogie bass figure, which is generally credited to Robert Johnson. He died November 22, 1968.

James "Son" Thomas was born in Eden (Yazoo County) on October 14, 1926. He learned to play guitar by listening to the radio. William Ferris helped to make Thomas known when he wrote about him in *Blues from the Delta.*

He toured Europe beginning in 1981 and made at least six more trips there. One of his last performances was the 1991 Delta Blues Festival in Greenville.

He was the last great Delta bluesman to play traditional acoustic guitar. His most famous songs were *Beef Stake Blues, Devil Blues,* and *Fast Boogie.* Thomas was also known for his sculpture in clay, which is on exhibit in Yale and Washington, D.C. He died on June 26, 1993.

Othar Turner was born in 1908 and resides in Gravel Springs. Turner started playing the fife at age sixteen. At that time, he saw R. E. Williams playing a fife and became interested. A fife is a hollow, flute-like instrument made from bamboo cane. Williams gave Turner fife lessons whenever it rained because they couldn't pick cotton. Williams also promised to give Turner a fife if he obeyed his mother. A month later, Turner received a new, homemade fife, compliments of Williams.

Othar Turner

Turner is one of the best fife players of all time. His band, The Risen Star Fife and Drum Band, consists of family members and friends.

In 1993, Turner first appeared on *Mississippi Blues in Memphis* Vol. 1. In 1993, he also recorded *Otha's Piece.* He recorded two singles, *Fife and Drum Piece* and *Glory Hallelujah.* He appeared on *Traveling Through the Jungle* and *It Came From Memphis.*

In 1996, Turner and The Risen Star Fife and Drum Band performed in Chicago at the 13th Annual Chicago Blues Fest. In 1998, he appeared on *The Alan Lomax Collection Sampler.*

Turner recorded his first album, *Everybody Hollerin' Goat,* which reached No. 2 on the *Billboard* charts in 1998. The album was recorded on his farm in Gravel Springs and named as one of the five "Essential Blues Records of the Decade." Also in 1998, Turner received the Miscellaneous Artist of the Year Award from *Billboard*. He released *Senegal to Senatobia* in 1999.

Walter Jacobs Vinson was born on February 2, 1901, near Bolton, learning guitar by age six. He played with the Mississippi Sheiks and in 1930 wrote one of the most popular tunes ever recorded, *Sitting on Top of the World.* Other songs included *Don't Wake Me Up, A Wonderful Thing, Tell Me to Do Right,* and *Isn't a Pain to Me.*

He died of pneumonia on April 22, 1975, in Chicago.

Booker T. Washington "Bukka" White was born in Houston, Texas, on November 12, 1906. Although born in Texas, he spent a significant amount of time in Mississippi. Many of his songs detail his experiences as a prisoner at Parchman Farm.

Bukka White

He played his guitar like a drum on train songs about his hobo life. This technique can be heard in a few of his classics, *Fixing To Die* and *Bukka's Jitterbug Swing*. He was influenced by Charlie Patton and sang in the tradition of Son House. He died in Memphis on February 26, 1977.

Robert Timothy Wilkins was born in Hernando on January 16, 1896. Wilkins was working as a Pullman porter in Memphis when he first recorded for Victor in 1928. His 1929 song *That's No Way to Get Along* was later recorded by The Rolling Stones as *Prodigal Son*.

Wilkins recorded a one-chord song called *Rollin' Stone*. In 1936, he quit blues because of a violent altercation at a house party where he was playing. He became a minister of the Church of God in Christ and remained so until his death in Memphis on May 26, 1987, at age ninety-one.

Joe Lee "Big Joe" Williams was born in Crawford on October 16, 1903. He played guitar, harmonica, accordion, and kazoo. In his early Delta days, he played work camps, jukes, store porches, streets, and alleys from New Orleans to Chicago. He recorded for five decades for Vocalion, OKeh, Paramount, Bluebird, and many other labels. Forty-six of his albums are available including *Back on My Feet, Bad Living, Big Fat Mama,* and *'71 Cadillac Blues*.

He died in Macon, Mississippi, on December 17, 1982.

"Sonny Boy" Williamson was born Aleck Ford "Rice" Miller in Glendora on December 5, 1899 (there is some confusion about his exact date of birth). He began guitar and harmonica at the age of five and was playing in juke joints and clubs throughout

Sonny Boy Williamson

41 • BLUES

Mississippi and Arkansas by age twenty under the name Little Boy Blue.

During the 1930s, he played at the Grand Ole Opry and worked with bluesmen like Elmore James, Robert Johnson, Howlin' Wolf, and Robert "Junior" Lockwood.

He took the name Sonny Boy Williamson in 1941 when he became a regular on the "King Biscuit Hour" radio show. Williamson and Lockwood were called the King Biscuit Entertainers. They joined with Peck Curtis, Dublow Taylor, and Pinetop Perkins to form a band by the same name.

Williamson didn't start recording until 1951 when he signed with Trumpet in Jackson, Mississippi. In 1955, he signed with the Checker Chess label and recorded with them until the early 1960s.

Williamson toured Europe as part of the American Negro Blues Festival with Willie Dixon, who was the talent coordinator, and Horst Lippman, the promoter. The tour talent included Muddy Waters, Howlin' Wolf, Lightnin' Hopkins, Lonnie Johnson, Sleepy John Estes, Big Joe Williams, Otis Spann, and others.

Later, Williamson returned to England to tour the college circuit with a young Eric Clapton and The Yardbirds as his backup band.

Williamson was one of the finest blues harmonica men who ever lived. He was a great influence on the English rhythm and blues scene and recorded with The Yardbirds, The Animals, and Jimmy Page. Ike Turner played piano for Williamson in 1942. His albums include *Sonny Boy Williamson* on Chess in 1958, *Bluebird Blues* on RCA in 1970, and *Portrait of a Blues Man* on Analogue in 1996.

He died in Helena, Arkansas, on May 25, 1965.

Johnny Young was born John O. Young in Vicksburg on January 1, 1918. He played the mandolin, an instrument more associated with bluegrass music than with the blues. His first hit was the Chicago blues classic *Money Taking Women*. Other songs include *All My Money Gone, Bad Blood, I'm Having a Ball, Mandown Boogie, Walking Slow,* and many others. Eight of his albums are available. He died in Chicago on April 18, 1974.

Classical

·····

Major achievements in classical music may seem a foreign possibility for a rural state like Mississippi. However, as far back as 1820, the state has produced some of the world's most beloved and well-known performers in classical music. Even more interesting, to some at least, is that many of these achievers are black.

Mississippi can be proud of its classical performers and composers. They have helped validate Mississippi as a haven of musical expression.

John Alexander was born in Meridian on October 21, 1923. He had a successful career as a tenor. He entered pre-med at Duke University and served with the U.S. Air Force. He then studied at the Cincinnati Conservatory with baritone Robert Weede.

He made his debut as Faust with the Cincinnati Opera in 1952 and joined the New York City Opera five years later. His first role was Alfredo.

His Metropolitan Opera debut, as Fernando, was on December 19, 1961. He had several successful European performances from 1967 to 1970. One of these was as Pollione in *Norma at Covent Garden* in England. This became one of his specialties, and he sang the part with some of the most celebrated Normas of the time, including Beverly Sills.

In May 1973, he accepted the title role in the first American performance of the original French version of *Don Carlos* which was staged by the Boston Opera. In 1974, he joined the faculty of the Cincinnati Conservatory.

Alexander was known for his versatility and for his great repertoire. He could sing in English, French, and German with little effort. His performances were known for good taste, fervor, stamina, and brilliant tone at the top of his range.

William Brown is a native of Jackson. He is a tenor who has performed with such prestigious orchestras as Boston, Cleveland, Cincinnati, Baltimore, Detroit, and London symphonies, and the New York and Royal Philharmonic orchestras.

Since his operatic debut with the Baltimore Opera Company, he has appeared with the New York Opera, the Florentine Opera Company, the Goldovsky Opera, Opera Ebony, Opera South, Rochester Opera Theater, and the Lake George Opera Festival.

He performed at Carnegie Hall for the eighty-fifth birthday celebration for Virgil Thomson. He made his third Carnegie appearance in January 1989 under the auspices of Today's Artists, Inc.

In the 1986-87 season, Brown was a guest soloist with the Brooklyn Philharmonic Orchestra's New York premier of William Bolcom's *Song of Innocence and Experience*. He was invited to participate in the Making Music Together festival in Moscow in 1991.

He is a charter member of the National Public Radio broadcast of the Black Music Research Ensemble.

In addition, Brown was seen and heard on CBS Television's "Sunday Morning" with Murry Sidlin and the New Haven Symphony Orchestra in a program which was rebroadcast on PBS. He has appeared on ABC, the NBC "Today Show," and the CBC Network in Canada.

Brown received an honorary Doctorate of Letters from Bridgewater State College of Massachusetts. He is a distinguished Professor of Voice at the University of North Florida in Jacksonville.

Ruby Pearl Elzy was born in Pontotoc on February 20, 1908. At age five, her father abandoned the family. Elzy's mother, Emma, single-handedly supported herself and her four children by working as a teacher in the Pontotoc Colored School, and by washing and ironing clothes for white families. As a child, Elzy learned Negro spirituals from her grandmother, who had been born a slave. Elzy began singing at age four in her church, and even as a child astonished people with the power and beauty of her voice.

Elzy was a freshman at Rust College in Holly Springs, Mississippi, where she was overheard singing in 1927 by a visiting college administrator, Dr. C. C. McCracken of Ohio State University. Overwhelmed by her natural talents, he arranged for her to transfer to Ohio State, where she graduated in 1930. Elzy then received a Rosenwald Fellowship to the Juilliard School in New York City, graduating in 1934.

Elzy made her Broadway debut in 1930 in the chorus of *Brown Buddies*. In 1933, she made her film debut as Dolly in *The Emperor Jones*, starring Paul Robeson. The screenwriter for that film was author DuBose Heyward. When Heyward and composer George Gershwin began working on *Porgy and Bess*, adapted from Heyward's novel, he recommended that Gershwin audition Elzy. After one hearing, Gershwin cast her as Serena. Elzy played Serena more than 800 times between the opera's 1935 premiere and her death in 1943, and introduced one of the opera's most famous arias, *My Man's Gone Now*. Elzy received tremendous acclaim in the role, both in the original Broadway production in 1935 and the 1942 revival, and on tour.

In addition to *Porgy and Bess*, Elzy starred on stage in *Run Little Chillun* and *John Henry*. She also sang in concerts and on radio. In 1937, she made her solo recital debut at New York's Town Hall and sang at the first Gershwin Memorial Concert at the Hollywood

Ruby Elzy, c. 1942.

•••••
Mississippi First:
RUBY ELZY, BORN IN PONTOTOC, PERFORMED THE FIRST "SERENA" ROLE IN THE OPERA, *PORGY AND BESS*.
•••••

Bowl, which was broadcast worldwide by CBS radio. Elzy received the greatest honor of her career in December, 1937, when she sang at the White House at the invitation of First Lady Eleanor Roosevelt. In addition to *The Emperor Jones,* Elzy appeared in four other films, most notably 1941's *Birth of the Blues* (with Bing Crosby and Mary Martin), in which she sang *St. Louis Blues.* In 1940, Elzy was chosen by composer Harold Arlen as one of the soloists to record the world premiere of *Reverend Johnson's Dream,* his original suite of American Negro spirituals.

A charter member of the Mississippi Musicians Hall of Fame, Elzy possessed one of the greatest soprano voices of her generation.

It was Elzy's dream to sing in grand opera, and she planned to make her operatic debut in the title role of *Aida* in 1944, following the close of the *Porgy and Bess* tour. Her dream, however, was to remain unfulfilled. On June 26, 1943, one week after singing her final performance as Serena in Denver, Colorado, Elzy died in Detroit, Michigan, following an operation. She was only 35 years old. Elzy is buried in her hometown of Pontotoc, Mississippi.

Elizabeth Taylor Greenfield was born a slave in Natchez in 1820. While still an infant, she was taken to Philadelphia, Pennsylvania, where she was adopted by a Quaker, Mrs. Greenfield, who paid for her musical training. She gained critical acclaim for her performance in *The Black Swan* and became known as the "Black Swan." She had a reputation for her sweet tones and wide vocal range.

Elizabeth's first musical debut was in 1851 in Buffalo, New York, where she sang before the Buffalo Musical Association. That performance established her as a major concert singer.

> **Mississippi First:**
> ELIZABETH TAYLOR GREENFIELD, THE "BLACK SWAN," WAS THE FIRST AFRICAN-AMERICAN CONCERT SINGER. SHE WAS BORN IN NATCHEZ.

After that, she was in demand as a performer nationally and internationally. In 1854, she performed before Queen Victoria at Buckingham Palace. After a concert career spanning some twenty years, she retired and opened a voice studio in Philadelphia.

She was recently inducted into the Mississippi Musicians Hall of Fame.

She died in 1876 in Philadelphia.

Benjamin Herrington was born in Pascagoula on September 3, 1964. He was raised in Columbia by parents who were music teachers. He graduated with performance honors from New England Conservatory, where he studied with John Swallow (co-founder of the New

York Brass Quintet), in 1986. He completed the Master's program at Juilliard in 1990 under the tutelage of Per Brevig (co-principal trombonist of the Metropolitan Opera).

In addition to his duties as co-founder and trombonist with the Meridian Arts Ensemble based in New York, Herrington maintains an active freelance career, performing with such groups as the New Haven Symphony, Continuum, in Broadway shows, and at the Marlboro Music Festival.

He has toured worldwide under the direction of Leonard Bernstein, Semyon Bychkov, James DePriest, and Christoph Eschenbach, and has collaborated with the American and New York Brass Quintets, the New York Trumpet Ensemble, and Philharmonia Virtuosi.

Herrington shares his experience and enthusiasm as a teacher for Juilliard's Music Advancement Program. A founding member of the Meridian Arts Ensemble, he currently resides in New York City and has recorded for Channel Classics, CRI, and Musical Heritage Society.

The Meridian Arts Ensemble has established itself as one of America's finest chamber ensembles through its innovative repertoire and critically acclaimed performances. Since its founding at the Juilliard School in 1987, it has established itself as one of America's finest young brass quintets having won four major competitions in a span of less than one year. Praised by the *Los Angeles Times* for its "near symphonic richness and depths," the ensemble first came to the attention of the music community as First Prize Winner of the 1990 Concert Artists Guild New York Competition. It has won special acclaim for its performances of a wide array of composers, ranging from J. S. Bach to Frank Zappa. It has performed several times on National Public Radio.

Recent albums include *Smart Went Crazy, Prime Meridian, Anxiety of Influence* and *Ear, Mind, I.*

Quincy Hilliard was born in Starkville on September 22, 1954. Hilliard was interested in music at an early age and was given lessons while in elementary school. His family was also musical.

Hilliard graduated from Starkville High School in 1972 and attended Mississippi State University (B.S., Music Ed.); Arkansas State University (M.A., Music Ed.); and the University of Florida for his Ph.D. in music theory and composition.

He is a well-known composer, conductor, professor, author, lecturer, and consultant. He is also the president of Hilliard Music Enterprise Inc., a personal consulting firm which has a board of noted music educators.

He is an associate professor of music theory and composition at the University of Southwestern Louisiana in Lafayette. He has taught at Florida International University and Nicholas State University. He has published several books, including *Selecting Music for the School Band, Theory Concepts Books 1 and 2,* and *Skill Builders Books 1 and 2.* He has written

Quincy Hilliard

articles for *Opera Journal, The Instrumentalist, School Musician, Band World, American Music Teacher, Florida Music Director,* and *Tennessee Musician.*

As a conductor, he is frequently invited to Mexico, Australia, and Canada to conduct, judge festivals, and to hold workshops. He was the conductor of the seventh annual Iowa Middle School Honor Band I in 1995.

He was commissioned by the Cultural Olympiad of the Atlanta Committee for the Olympic Games to write a composition for the 1996 Olympics. The composition is entitled *Anthem for Victory.*

Hilliard composes music for bands and has had more than seventy published compositions. His first published piece was *Furioso* in 1980. One of his best-known works, *Ghost Dance,* was based upon an historical event. It was premiered at the Kennedy Center for the Performing Arts and received a standing ovation. He was also invited to guest conduct *Ghost Dance* at the University of Saskatchewan in Canada at its 1994 Music Festival.

Hilliard has been honored with several awards. He has been honored by the American Society of Composers, Authors and Publishers for 1996-97, the ninth time that he has received the honor.

He received the National Bandmasters Association Citation of Excellence Award in 1990 and the National Catholic Bandmaster Service Award in 1991. The University of Southwestern Louisiana awarded him the Heymann Endowed Professorship in Music in 1995.

Samuel Jones was born on June 2, 1935, in Inverness. While still in high school, he was composing music; one of his compositions for band was played by the Lions All-State Band. He graduated from Central High School in Jackson and received his undergraduate degree with highest honors from Millsaps College.

He acquired his professional training at the Eastman School of Music, where he earned his M.A. and Ph.D. degrees in composition under Howard Hanson, Bernard Rogers, and Wayne Barlow.

Jones first came into prominence as a conductor, one of the few Americans to advance through the ranks of the smaller American orchestras and become conductor of one of the majors (the Rochester Philharmonic). He then achieved national recognition in another field as he founded Rice University's Shepherd School of Music, a significant new music school. He served for six years as its first dean.

After stepping down as dean at the Shepherd School, Jones continued as Professor of Composition and Conducting and Director of Graduate Studies. After twenty-four years at Rice, he retired in 1997. He and his wife moved to the Seattle area where he was appointed by Gerard Schwarz as Composer in Residence of the Seattle Symphony.

Jones is the recipient of numerous awards and prizes for his compositions, including a Ford Foundation Recording/Publication Award, a Martha Baird Rockefeller Grant, NEA Grants, repeated ASCAP Awards, an International Angel Award, and the 1986 and 1991 Music Awards from the Mississippi Institute of Arts and Letters. He received an honorary doctorate from Millsaps College in May, 2000.

His works have been performed by such orchestras as the Philadelphia Orchestra, the Seattle Symphony, the Detroit Symphony, the Utah Symphony, the Houston Symphony, the Cincinnati Symphony, the New Orleans Philharmonic, the Rochester Philharmonic, and scores of others. His music has been commissioned by, among others, the Houston Symphony, the Seattle Symphony, the American Symphony Orchestra League, the Amarillo Symphony, the Midland-Odessa Symphony, the Sioux City Symphony, the Saginaw Symphony, Millsaps College, the Mississippi Boys Choir, and the Choral Society of Greensboro.

A former conducting student of Richard Lert and William Steinberg, his numerous conducting credits include tenures as Conductor of the Rochester Philharmonic, Music Advisor of the Flint Symphony, and Music Director of the Saginaw Symphony as well as guest engagements with many orchestras including, among others, the Detroit Symphony, the Houston Symphony, the Pittsburgh Symphony, the Buffalo Philharmonic, the Prague Symphony, and the Iceland Symphony. Early in his career he founded the Alma Symphony and the Delta College Summer Festival of Music in Michigan. His compositions include three symphonies and many other orchestral works, as well as works for chorus and orchestra, opera, and chamber groups. His music is published by Carl Fischer, Inc., and Campanile Music Press and recorded by Naxos,

Samuel Jones

CRI, Gasparo, and Centennial Records.

Jones was recently inducted into the Mississippi Musicians Hall of Fame.

Willard Aldrich Palmer was born January 31, 1917, in McComb. He attended Whitworth College in Brookhaven and Millsaps College in Jackson. During this time, he continued to play the accordion as a soloist and with various prominent local ensembles. After World War II, he and his former student, the late Bill Hughes, formed a partnership that was to become the team that produced the largest-selling accordion course in the world.

Palmer became a world-renowned musician, scholar, and music teacher. His revolutionary teaching principles were the subject of *Willard A. Palmer's Contributions to Piano Pedagogy,* doctoral dissertation by Kathleen L. Schubert, Ph.D. He wrote 789 published works, including an accordion method, several piano methods, a method for Hammond Chord Organ, a guitar method, hundreds of solo pieces, and many choral works.

His works have been translated into German, Japanese, French, Dutch, and Spanish. All of these works were published by Alfred Publishing Company.

At the University of Houston, he and Bill Hughes formed two ensembles that were of major importance: the Concert Trio, two accordions and a bass viol, and the Palmer-Hughes Accordion Symphony which played in Carnegie Hall. Both of these groups played serious classical music and music from Broadway musicals.

Willard Palmer

His later years were dedicated to research into classical and baroque music and into teaching methods. He was recognized worldwide as an authority on Baroque music ornamentation. His work in this field was the basis of the Alfred Masterworks Series of publications, now recognized as the best publication in this field.

Palmer was also an inventor. When he was a child, he invented the now universally used turn signal indicator for automobiles, which worked by causing the tail lights to blink. Later in college, he and his close friend Fred Bush invented a navigation device that would indicate both the air and ground speeds of an airplane and a device that would theoretically allow a bombardier to place a bomb on target with pinpoint accuracy. Palmer and Bush sent these to the U.S. Government with their compliments. Later he learned that both components were used by the Air Corps and the latter device became known as the Norden Bombsight.

His other inventions include several for the accordion which allow the traditional Stradella bass buttons to be played as single notes, this permitting the accordionist to play major symphonic and piano works exactly as written. He held doctoral degrees in humanities, music, and music education and masters degrees in music and music education. He was the recipient of many awards, including the American Accordionists' Convention which honored him for his work for the instrument.

He died on April 30, 1996.

Mary Violet Leontyne Price, better known as Leontyne Price, was born in Laurel on February 10, 1927. Leontyne is hailed by *Time Magazine* as the "diva di tutte le dive," or diva of all the divas.

She sang in the choir at St. Paul's Methodist Church in Laurel, as did her mother, Kate (Baker) Price. Her father James Price was a sawmill worker.

Price began piano lessons at the age of five, and had her first recital at six. She attended Sandy Gavin Elementary where she learned dancing and acrobatics. When Price was nine, her mother took her to a Marian Anderson concert in Jackson and young Price was inspired.

While attending Oak Park High School, Price sang first soprano with the Oak Park Choral group and later graduated with honors in 1944. Price then enrolled in Industrial Arts (Central State College) in Wilberforce, Ohio, where she studied music education.

Price won a four-year scholarship to New York's Juilliard School of Music in 1949. During her four years at Juilliard, Price studied singing, stage presence, acting, and makeup. She appeared in many of Juilliard's operatic productions. During one of her performances, she was seen and heard by composer Virgil Thomson, who gave her career its start. Thomson asked her to sing the role of St. Cecilia in the opera, *Four Saints in Three Acts,* which was her first appearance as a

> •••••
> **Mississippi First:**
> LEONTYNE PRICE, BORN IN LAUREL, WAS HAILED BY *TIME MAGAZINE* AS THE "DIVA DI TUTTE LE DIVE" OR "DIVA OF ALL THE DIVAS." SHE WAS ALSO THE FIRST OPERA SINGER TO BE AWARDED THE PRESIDENTIAL MEDAL OF FREEDOM.
> •••••

professional singer. Price began touring the United States and Europe and her debut in Paris in 1952 was followed by tours in Vienna, Berlin, and London. Her operatic debut in 1955 was broadcast coast-to-coast by NBC-TV Opera Company.

Four Saints in Three Acts was very successful, and this helped Price land the role of Bess in the folk opera, *Porgy and*

Leontyne Price, Diva of all the Divas.

Bess. In 1957 at the San Francisco opera, Price sang in the opera, *Dialogues of the Camelites.* Price got her first chance to play the role of Aida because the opera singer who was scheduled to sing became ill. Price's outstanding performance in Verdi's *Il Trovatore* at the Met received a standing ovation of forty-two minutes.

Price appeared in 118 Metropolitan Opera productions between 1961 and 1969. In Samuel Barber's opera, *Antony and Cleopatra,* Price sang and played the role of Cleopatra to sold-out houses.

In 1970, Price curtailed her operatic appearances and concentrated on concert recitals and recording sessions. During Price's career she has won nearly twenty Grammy Awards. Price's retirement from the opera stage came in 1985 with the performance of *Aida* at the Lincoln Center. Price has also written *Aida: A Picture Book for All Ages.* She has performed at presidential inaugurations and sung before the Pope. In 1991, she sang at Carnegie Hall's one-hundredth anniversary.

Although she is no longer making recordings, BMG/RCA has recently released a new boxed set entitled *The Essential Leontyne Price.* It includes eleven CDs of Price's greatest and rarest recorded performances from operatic scenes, arias, art songs, spirituals, and sacred songs.

Price was named as "A Remarkable American Woman: 1776-1976" by *Life Magazine.* She is the first opera singer to receive America's highest civilian award, the Presidential Medal of Freedom, which was given to her by President Lyndon Johnson.

President Ronald Reagan presented her with her first Medal of Arts. The government of France named her a Commandeur of the French Order of Arts and Letters, and the Republic of Italy bestowed upon her its Order of Merit.

Leontyne Price was recently inducted into the Mississippi Musicians Hall of Fame.

Steve Rouse was born in Moss Point in 1953 and began composing and improvising at age five, later studying piano, bassoon, and saxophone. At thirteen, he began four years as a bassoonist in the Gulf Coast Symphony and also began performing with his first rhythm and blues group.

His principal composition teachers include Luigi Zaninelli at the University of Southern Mississippi and, at the University of Michigan where he received his Master of Music and Doctorate of Music in composition, Leslie Bassett and William Albright.

At the conclusion of his graduate studies, his *Hexachords and Their Trichordal Generators: An Introduction* was published in the music theory journal *In Theory Only* in December 1985.

In 1988, Rouse joined the theory and composition faculty of the University of Louisville School of Music, where he coordinates the collaborative School of Music/Louisville Orchestra New Dimensions Series. Since 1989, Rouse has served as a first round juror for the Grawemeyer International Composition Award. He has also been a National Advisory Board member for the League of Composers/International Society for Contemporary Music since 1991.

Winner of the 1987 Prix de Rome, Rouse holds among his awards a Meet the Composer residency, a National Endowment for the Arts Composition Fellowship, the American Academy and Institute of Arts and Letters 1995 Hinrichsen Prize, 1985 Ives Composition Prize, two Al Smith Artist Fellowships from the Kentucky Arts Council, First Prize in the 1986 Dartmouth Competition for New Choral Music for his *Dense Pack,* and numerous ASCAP awards.

Rouse's works have been performed in England, Italy, Ecuador, the Soviet Union, Taiwan, and throughout the U.S. This includes performances by the St. Louis Symphony the Cincinnati Symphony, the Louisville Orchestra, the Detroit Symphony, the American Composers Orchestra, the American Brass Quintet, Parnassus, Composers, Inc., and the League/ISCM.

He received a commission to compose music from, among others, the Louisville Orchestra; the League/ISCM, the Guayaquil; Ecuador Chamber Orchestra; the University of Michigan Contemporary Directions Ensemble for the 1984 National Organ Conference; and the Kentucky Music Teachers Association. Rouse's *Into the Light* has been recorded for Telarc Records by the Cincinnati Symphony; and his *Enigma* for Delos Records by Gerard Schwarz and the Seattle Symphony, with trumpet soloist Jeff Silberschlag. His trumpet sonata, *The Avatar,* as recorded by Ray Mase, is available on Summit Records. *More Light, The Avatar,* and *A Flying Leap!* have been recorded for the Coronet label by trumpeter Michael Tunnell. Rouse is published by C. F. Peters, MMB, and Primal Press.

James Sclater is from Mobile, Alabama, but has spent his professional career in Mississippi. Sclater received his bachelor of music and master's degrees from the University of Southern Mississippi and his doctorate from the University of Texas.

Sclater has been a faculty member of Mississippi College in Clinton since 1970 and has written more than ninety musical works, many of which have been published and performed.

He received the American Society of Composers, Authors and Publishers (ASCAP) Award for the 1999-2000 school year, which made the ninth consecutive year for this award. The award is designed to encourage writers of serious music.

It is because of a Russian arts administrator that Sclater's music is now being heard around the world. The director of Cherepovets Children's Theater in Russia requested copies of Sclater's work, and it was performed in Russia at the children's theater.

His composition *Kinderscenen* has been performed on Danish National Radio;

and his work, *Concerto of Orchestra,* has been performed by the Irish Radio Orchestra.

William Grant Still was born May 11, 1895, in Woodville. Still was the only child of Carrie "Frambo" Still and William Grant Still, Sr. Still was of African-American descent but his ancestry also consisted of Scotch-Irish, Spanish, and Cherokee. Both of Still's parents were teachers at Alabama A&M College in Huntsville, Alabama.

Young Still's father died before he was four months; and William was nine or ten years of age when his widowed mother married Charles B. Shepperson, also a lover of music.

Mrs. Still knew her young son had a musical gift when he began to make toy violins. It was then that she decided to pay for his violin lessons. Still began writing music at age sixteen and graduated as valedictorian in his class. Taking his mother's advice, Still attended Wilberforce University in Ohio to major in science.

After years of completing courses as a science major, he realized he was more interested in music. As a result, Still joined the Wilberforce University String Quartet. He began arranging and composing for the school band, and as a bandleader, he learned to play different instruments so that he could teach others how to play.

By Still's senior year at Wilberforce, he decided that he was unwilling to give up his amateur musical career. Therefore, in 1916, at twenty-one, Still left Wilberforce University and enrolled at Oberlin College's Conservatory of Music. He did not earn a degree at Oberlin but went to New York to work professionally. Still's pay was not nearly enough to support himself so he worked as a waiter and a janitor.

In 1918, Still joined the United States Navy and served in World War I. After his release from the navy, he became an arranger and musician for W. C. Handy. He created the band's first arrangement of *St. Louis Blues* and *Beale Street Blues.*

Still got experience working with Duke Ellington and Paul Whiteman. He wrote seven operas, eight symphonies, ballets, chamber music, chorus music, and orchestra works. Still released a poem called *Darker America* in 1924; it was such a success he wrote *From the Black Belt,* which was based on short story sketches.

Still played in the pit bands for musical shows and became the bandleader at the Plantation Club. He wrote arrangements for many entertainers, but his composing did not stop. *Sahdji,* a two-act ballet based on an African story, was released in 1930. *Africa,* a poem, was also a work of his in 1930. In 1931, his most popular work was published, *Afro-American Symphony*. It was the first major piece by an African-American to be accepted by the American musical establishment.

Some called Still's music "Negro-music" and he disliked the term because he felt that having a black person compose and write music did not make it "Negro-music." He experienced racism and discrimination but disagreed with the notion that blacks could not succeed in the music world.

In New York City, Still led a radio orchestra of white men, the first for blacks. Still was also the first black to arrange and record a fantasy on *St. Louis Blues*.

He released other works such as *Kaintuck* (1935), a concerto, and *Lenox Avenue* (1936), a ballet about life in Harlem. In 1936, Still was the first black conductor to lead a major American orchestra, appearing with the Rochester Philharmonic at the Hollywood Bowl.

Many other works of Still's include *And They Lynched Him on a Tree* (1940), *A Bayou Legend* (1940), *Pastorela* (1946), and *To You America!* (1952). Still created many musical shows, but the ones produced were *Troubled Island, Highway No. 1. U.S.A.*, and *Bayou Legend*.

Still received The Cincinnati Symphony Orchestra Prize and the Cleveland Symphony Prize. He was given honorary degrees from colleges such as Howard University, Bates College, and Oberlin College. Wilberforce awarded him a diploma of honor and an honorary Master of Music degree in 1936.

Still was awarded the National Federation of Music Clubs Prize and also received a commission to write the theme music for the first New York World's Fair. A Guggenheim Fellowship and Governor's Outstanding Mississippian Award were also given to him. He was recently inducted into the

William Grant Still

> ·····
> ## Mississippi First:
> WILLIAM GRANT STILL, BORN IN WOODVILLE, WAS THE FIRST AFRICAN-AMERICAN COMPOSER TO HAVE A SYMPHONY PERFORMED BY A MAJOR AMERICAN ORCHESTRA. HE IS CALLED THE "DEAN OF AFRICAN-AMERICAN COMPOSERS."
> ·····

Mississippi Musicians Hall of Fame.

A William Grant Still Symposium was held at St. Augustine's College in Raleigh, North Carolina in 1995, almost twenty years after his death.

Still died on December 3, 1978, of heart failure. In 1981, *A Bayou Legend* was produced for PBS; and in 1984 the premiere of *Minette Fontaine* was given by the Baton Rouge Opera Company. Today Duke University has an exhibit of William Grant Still's work in its Special Collections Library.

Dr. Walter J. Turnbull was born in Greenville. He is an honors graduate of Tougaloo College, where his achievements earned him recognition in Who's Who in American Colleges and Universities.

He has celebrated thirty years as the leader of the internationally acclaimed Boys Choir of Harlem, Inc. Under his leadership, The Boys Choir of Harlem has evolved from a small church choir to a world renowned artistic and educational institution.

He has built an innovative program which addresses the social, educational, and emotional needs of urban boys and girls. The experience helps them transform their lives through music. The Boys Choir of Harlem Inc., helps children achieve their creative potential, build self esteem, and find positive role models. The children develop a strong value system of discipline and hard work in preparation for the future.

A talented performing artist in his own right, Turnbull made his operatic debut with the Houston Grand Opera in Scott Joplin's *Treemonisha*. He has performed in *Carmen* and *Turandot* with Opera South and created the role of Antonio in the world premiere of Roger Ames' opera *Amistad*.

His other operatic roles include Alfredo in *La Traviata* and Tamino in *Die Zauberflote,* both with the Lake George Opera. He performed in *Carmina Burana* with the Alvin Ailey Dance Theatre and reprised his role in Joplin's *Treemonisha* on Broadway. He appeared as a tenor soloist with the New York Philharmonic and the Philadelphia Orchestra. He also sang with the Godovsky Opera Theatre and Young Audiences, Inc.

In addition to his role as Principal Conductor of The Boys Choir of Harlem, Turnbull gives recitals at Merkin Hall in New York City. He holds master classes for artistic and educational organizations throughout the country and lectures frequently on education and the arts.

Turnbull is the recipient of numerous awards and recognitions, most recently the 1998 Heinz Award in the Arts and Humanities. He has been honored by the State of New York and the State of Mississippi. He has received the William M. Sullivan Award, the Eleanor Roosevelt Community Service Award, the Edwin Berry National Business and Professional Award, the Black Book Publishers Award, the Mayor's Voluntary Action Award, the New Yorker for New York Award, and the National Association of Negro Musicians prize.

He was awarded the President's Volunteer Action Award, the Intrepid Freedom Award, the Actors Equity Association LeNoire Award, Chase Manhattan Humanitarian Recognition Award, and the NAACP Man of Action Award. He was named "One of the 15 Greatest Men on Earth" by *McCall's Magazine*.

In 1997, Turnbull and The Boys Choir of Harlem were awarded the prestigious National Medal of Arts. In 1998 he received the *Readers Digest* American Heroes in Education Award and was named one of the New York Black 100 by the Schomburg Center for Research in Black Culture.

Turnbull has been frequently profiled in the media. He has been featured on "Today," "CBS This Morning," "Good Morning, America," "Nightline," "20/20," "48 Hours," and "60 Minutes." He has also been featured on CNN, UPN News, and the Fox News Network. He has appeared on "Amazing Grace with Bill Moyers," "Great Performances: Ellington and his Music" and "Pavarotti in Central Park." He is the author of a highly acclaimed book, *Lift Every Voice: Expecting the Most and Getting the Best from All of God's Children*.

He received his Master's in Music and Doctor of Musical Arts degrees from the Manhattan School of Music. He graduated from the Institute for Non-Profit Management at the Columbia University School of Business and has received honorary degrees from California State University, Hofstra, Mannes College of Music, Muhlenberg College, Queens College, Skidmore, and Tougaloo. Tougaloo has named a scholarship in his honor for The Boys Choir of Harlem, Inc., graduates.

Turnbull is featured in an article in *Reader's Digest* (June 2000) entitled "There's Joy in Harlem."

Country Music

Country music has often been called the music of America and Mississippi the birthplace of country music. Mississippi has contributed some of the most respected and recognized musicians in this field. From Jimmie Rodgers, the Father of Country Music, to Tammy Wynette, the First Lady of Country Music, the natives of Mississippi have spanned the decades in country music. Taking influences from blues, jazz, and gospel, country music is a meshing of all things American.

Earl Poole Ball was born in 1940 in Columbia and began to take piano from his aunt at age eight. In high school, he played in a hillbilly band at local VFW and American Legion halls. This work led to a regular spot on the popular Jimmy Swan TV program in Hattiesburg.

From there, Ball decided to try his luck in Houston, Texas. He had only a $100 bill that his dad had given him. When he arrived, he found work at Houston's Silver Dollar Lounge, where he met Mickey Gilley. Gilley helped co-produce a Ball album with Kenny Rogers' brother Leland.

Playing in Houston provided no real opportunities for Ball so he moved to Los Angeles and found work playing in the Aces Club as well as other clubs in San Bernadino and Fontana. Ball had a small movie part in *Country A-Go-Go* with Eddie Hodges.

During his ongoing residency at the Aces Club, Ball met guitar great Joe Maphis, who was just one of the dozens of country and western music legends attracted to the club by the extended jam sessions. Greats like Waylon Jennings, Roger Miller, Hank Cochran, and Gram Parsons all played with Ball at one time or another. Between gigs at the Aces and doing contract work composing songs for Hollywood's Central Songs, Ball met drummer Jerry Wiggins.

Buck Owens called Ball on Jerry Wiggins' recommendation and that led to Ball's playing on a number of sessions with the Buckaroos, including those albums that yielded hits such as *Got You on My Mind Again, Who's Gonna Mow Your Grass,* and *Big in Vegas.*

Ball eventually landed session work with Gram Parsons' short-lived International Submarine Band. This job reunited him with old friend John Camail and helped him get work with Parsons, who is most known for *Sweetheart of the Rodeo* and The Flying Burrito Brothers.

By 1969, things were changing at Capitol Records and Ball was transferred to Nashville. He became a house producer alongside such heavy hitters as Billy Shrill and Larry Butler, and was soon assigned to Freddie Hart. Hart had a hit, *Easy Lovin'.* It was a bit of a test, producing an album by a singer who just had a monster hit, but Ball's session produced *My Hangup Is You,* which occupied the No. 1 spot on the country charts for six weeks.

In Nashville, Ball met Harlan Howard, who introduced him to Johnny Cash. A relationship was forged that lasted twenty years.

Ball produced Cash's landmark 1977 LP *Rockabilly Blues,* but it was the last such production job he would assume. Ball stuck by the singer until Cash's decision to retire from the road in 1997 due to the debilitating effects of Shy-Drager syndrome.

It was Ball's partnership with Cash that led his career in another direction entirely when film director Peter Bogdanovich expressed interest in using *I Don't Think I Can Take You Back Again* for his 1981 comedy, *They All Laughed.* The director needed a country band and brought Ball into the production. Ball began taking acting classes and immediately found himself in a TV movie with Cash and Brenda Vaccaro, *The Pride of Jesse Hallum*. The two appeared together again in 1983's fact-based *Murder in Coweta County*, starring Andy Griffith as a businessman convinced he's gotten away with murder and Cash as the lawman determined to get him.

By this time, music was taking a lesser role and acting taking more time, so Ball moved back to California in 1986 to pursue more movie roles. He continued acting, taking a role on the long-running daytime drama, "The Young and the Restless," and later he teamed up with Bogdanovich again for a feature role in 1988's *Texasville*.

He shared the screen with Samantha Mathis and River Phoenix as well as Sandra Bullock, K. T. Oslin, Trisha Yearwood, Jimmie Dale Gilmore, and Pam Tillis in 1993's *The Thing Called Love*. His last film was *The Naked City: A Killer Christmas*, in which he played an evil Santa Claus pursued by lawman Scott Glenn.

Ball continues to perform and tour.

Marion F. Bandy, Jr., better known as Moe, was born on February 12, 1944, in Meridian. He moved to San Antonio, Texas, when he was six and later became a rodeo cowboy.

Bandy decided to sing and play in his father's band, the Mission City Playboys. By 1962, he formed his own band called Moe and the Mavericks. He played clubs and some television in Texas, but kept his day job as a sheet metal worker.

In 1973, he made his first recording with Ray Baker of Nashville, *I Just Started Hatin' Cheatin' Songs Today*. The song hit the charts at No. 5. He had several successful songs such as *It Was So Easy, Bandy The Rodeo Clown, You Wrote My Life, Here I Am, Drunk Again,* and *I'm Sorry For You, My Friend*.

He teamed with Joe Stampley and produced such duets as *Just Good Ole Boys* and *Hey Joe, Hey Moe*. Bandy and Stampley won duo awards from the Country Music Association and the Academy of Country Music in 1979.

Bandy made regular appearances at the Grand Ole Opry and toured extensively throughout the United States and Europe. He stayed true to traditional country, not wanting to cross the pop lines.

Since 1974, Bandy has had more than thirty Top 10 singles. His 1979 single *It's A Cheatin' Situation* won the ACM's Song of the Year honor in 1980. In 1987, he achieved acclaim again with *Till I'm Too Old To Die Young,* and *You Haven't Heard The Last of Me*. He opened his own theater in Branson, Missouri, in 1991 called Moe Bandy Americana Theater. He and the Americana Band perform two shows daily, Monday through Saturday.

Bucky Barrett was born in 1943 in Canton and is now the driving force behind ARRA, a creative production company in Nashville. Yet he may be best known as an acoustic and electric guitarist. He has performed on more than 1,500 albums with acclaimed artists such as Roy Orbison, Marty Robbins, Ray Charles, Neil Young, Dottie West, Barbara Mandrell, Willie Nelson, Chet Atkins, Bobby Vinton, Boxcar Willie, Charlie Daniels, and many others.

His network TV performances include "The Tonight Show," "Late Show," "Saturday Night Live," and "The Today Show." He has worked and composed for TV and written jingles for Coca-Cola, Dr. Pepper, Chrysler Motor Cars, McDonald's, Burger King, Pizza Hut, and Toyota.

He has performed live with Roy Orbison, Tanya Tucker, Ronnie Milsap, Conway Twitty, Little Jimmy Dickens, Johnny Paycheck, and other top talents.

He has won national awards such as a Grammy with Roy Orbison for Best Country Collaboration (1989), Instrumentalist of Year Nomination by Country Music Association (1984) and Best Studio Guitarist Nominations every year from 1980 to 1985.

His recordings include *Killin' the Wind*, *The Nashville Super Pickers*, and *Mississippi Morning*. His more recent albums include *Long Time Coming*, twelve songs played on gut-string guitar, and *Twelve Songs of Christmas*.

Henry "Hank" Cochran was born in Greenville on August 2, 1935. When he was in his late teens, he moved to New Mexico and two years later to California. While in California he started working at local clubs which lead him to local radio and television appearances.

Soon Cochran teamed up with Eddie Cochran (no relation) in a duo called The Cochran Brothers, but left the group in 1958. Cochran became a regular on a television show called "The California Hayride."

He moved to Nashville in 1960 and by 1961 had become successful both as a singer and songwriter. With Harlan Howard, he worked on a song that became No. 1 in 1961—*I Fall to Pieces* sung by the great Patsy Cline. That same year, he signed with Liberty Records and released *Sally Was A Good Girl*.

In 1962, five of his songs were in the Top 10. Patsy Cline's *She Got You*; Burl Ives' *A Little Bitty Tear* and *Funny Way of Laughing*; Eddy Arnold's *Tears Broke Out on Me*; Shirley Collie and Willie Nelson's record of *Willingly*; and Ray Price's 1963 hit, *Make the World Go Away*, were all written by Cochran.

In 1965, the Victor label produced the LP, *Hank Cochran*, and in 1966, he recorded his own version of some of his best-selling songs on *Hits From the Heart*. Cochran enjoyed a wide range of successes. Though he is probably better known

Bucky Barrett

PHOTO COURTESY OF NANCY JACOBS

Hank Cochran

as a songwriter, he is also quite an accomplished singer.

Paul Davis was born in Meridian on April 21, 1948. The biggest hits he wrote and recorded were *I Go Crazy* (No. 7 in 1977 and 1978); *'65 Love Affair* (No. 6 in 1982); a No. 1 with Marie Osmond, *You're Still New To Me* (1986); and a No. 1 with Tanya Tucker and Paul Overstreet, *I Won't Take Less than Your Love* (1987). Davis wrote the No. 1 country hit *Meet Me In Montana* (1986). He has recorded eight albums including *Like A Little Bit of Paul Davis* (1972) and *Cool Night* (1981). He produced many hits for other artists.

Davis could also be classified as a rock musician with a laid-back and mellow delivery.

Steve Forbert was born in 1955 in Meridian. At age ten, Forbert started playing guitar (later singing and playing harmonica). After attending junior college and working as a truck driver, he moved to New York City at the age of 21. There, he performed for spare change in Grand Central Station before working his way up to the Manhattan club circuit.

After signing with Nemperor, Forbert debuted in 1978 with *Alive on Arrival,* which earned critical acclaim for its taut, poetic lyrics. Anointed "the new Dylan" upon his recording debut, folk-rock singer/songwriter Forbert continued his rise. 1979's *Jackrabbit Slim* was his most successful album, reaching the Top 20 on the strength of the hit single *Romeo's Tune.*

However, both 1980's *Little Stevie Orbit* and a self-titled 1982 effort did poorly, and Forbert was dropped by his label. He spent much of the decade in Nashville, where he continued improving his song writing skills and performed regularly throughout the South. In 1988, Garry Tallent produced Forbert's comeback album, *Streets of This Town.* Pete Anderson took over the production reins in 1992 on *The American in Me,* but Forbert's continued lack of chart success prompted the label to cut him. After 1994's live effort *Be Here Now,* he recorded *Mission of the Crossroad Palms* for Giant the next year. *Rocking Horse Head* followed in 1996, and in early 2000 Forbert returned with *Evergreen Boy.*

Forbert worked with Bobby Hicks, Hugh McDonald, Barry Lazarowitz, Robbie Kondor, Bill Jones, Garry Tallent,

Danny Counts, Roger Clark, Steve Burgh, David Sanborn, Bob Wray, and many others.

Some of his albums include *Alive on Arrival* (1978) on Nemperor; *Jackrabbit Slim* (1979) on Nemperor; *In Concert Live* (1996) on BMG; and his tenth album, *Evergreen Boy* (2000) on Koch.

Bobbie Gentry was born Roberta Lee Streeter in Chickasaw County on July 27, 1944. She moved to Greenwood when she was six years old. Gentry wrote and sang the No. 1 hit record *Ode To Billy Joe* in 1967. It earned her three Grammys that year. The song was made into a movie of the same title in 1976 and was filmed in Mississippi.

Her album, *Ode to Billy Joe,* went gold in 1967 as did the album *Bobbie Gentry and Glen Campbell* in 1969. The Academy of Country Music voted her Most Promising Female Vocalist for 1967. She has recorded eight albums. She married singer Jim Stafford on October 15, 1978.

Bobbie Gentry

Mickey Gilley was born in Natchez around 1936. He grew up in Ferriday, Louisiana with his cousins Jerry Lee Lewis and Jimmy Stewart. All three boys would sneak off to blues joints at night to learn more about music.

Gilley's mother, who made only $18 a week, saved enough to buy them a piano when Gilley was ten. During his teen years, Gilley became a good piano player. After he heard a song by cousin Jerry Lee Lewis, Gilley decided to pursue music as well.

He worked in recording studios near Houston, Texas playing the piano in local clubs. Eventually he became popular enough to play around the United States working for small record labels before being signed by Dot Records.

Around the early 1970s, Gilley and Sherwood Cryer, an old friend of Gilley's, opened a club called Gilley's in Pasadena, Texas, which seated 5,000. It was called the world's largest honky-tonk and Gilley regularly performed there. In 1980 the club was chosen for a setting in the movie *Urban Cowboy.* This made Gilley's a popular attraction for tourists, but the club was later burned down by an angry young man.

Gilley was featured on a biography that aired on TNN, "The Life and Times of Mickey Gilley." He received the Academy of Country Music Award for Single Record of the Year, *Bring It On Home* in 1976. His first hit was *Room Full of Roses* (1974) followed by 17 number-one hits such as *I Overlooked An Orchid* and *Stand By Me* that also went Pop (#22 in 1980).

Mickey Gilley

Gilley now lives in Branson, Missouri, where he has a theater which seats 950 people. He plays there nine months of the year.

Faith Hill was born in 1967 in Star as Audrey Faith Perry. She began to sing as soon as she could talk, joined her first band when she was seventeen, and moved to Nashville when she was nineteen.

When in Nashville, Hill worked as a receptionist at Gary Morris Publishing Company. In fear of losing her job, she kept her singing a secret. But one day her secret was revealed when David Chase heard her singing. He encouraged her to record a demo called *It Scares Me*.

She later sang harmony with Gary Burr on one of his shows at the Bluebird Cafe. Soon she was a regular back-up singer, which allowed A&R Records Senior Vice President Martha Sharp to hear her.

Sharp later listened to the demo tape of Hill with Gary Burr and was impressed enough to contact heavyweight producer Scott Hendricks.

In 1993, Hill's debut single, *Wild One*, reached the No. 1 spot and stayed there four weeks. No other country female singer had accomplished that feat since Connie Smith in 1964.

Hill's second single, *Piece of My Heart*, went to No. 1 in September 1993, and her first full-length album, *Take Me As I Am*, was certified gold in October 1993. She is known for such titles as *Go The Distance* and *I've Got This Friend*. In May 1994, Hill received the Academy of Country Music Award for Best New Female Vocalist. She was also nominated for CMA's Horizon Award.

Hill has appeared on "The Late Show" with David Letterman, "Today Show," "The Tonight Show," and "Hot Country Jam." She has also toured extensively with Reba McEntire, Brooks and Dunn, and Alan Jackson. Faith has been featured in *USA Today*, *Entertainment Weekly*, *Los Angeles Times*, *Chicago Tribune*, and countless other publications.

On July 4, 1994, she performed in front of almost half a million people for "A Capitol Fourth" on PBS. She released her second album, *The Road to Nashville*, in the fall of 1995. It tells the story of a young girl's dream of performing at the

Faith Hill

Grand Ole Opry; Hollywood star, Julia Roberts, provides narration on the album between the songs.

In 1999, Hill and her husband Tim McGraw cemented their claim as the new king and queen of country music by taking home awards in six categories in the TNN Music City News Country Awards. Hill was named Best Female Vocalist and her hit *This Kiss* won Best Video and Best Single.

In May 2000, she won Best Female Vocalist from the Academy of Country Music Awards. She also won top honors for her music video *Breathe*.

In January 2001, Hill won three American Music Awards: Favorite Female Artist (Rock and Pop Music), Favorite Female Artist (Country Music), and Favorite Country Album (*Breathe*).

Hill is now seen on TV as a model, advertising spokesperson, and documentary subject.

Jimmy Johnson was born in Canton but raised in Starkville where his father was superintendent of schools. His parents tell the story of his scooting his playpen across the floor to be closer to the radio at age nine months.

Johnson played the trumpet in his high school band and the guitar with a rock band. At nineteen, he changed to electric bass and played in The Knights and Ravin' Blue bands at Mississippi State University. He stayed with blues and rhythm and blues until the Beatles came along.

He and his wife, Patricia Lyon, went to Memphis in the late 1960s where Johnson played R&B and soul. He moved to Nashville in 1974 where played with Jerry Reed. He was road manager and bandleader for Lynne Anderson.

Johnson has had a long association with Vince Gill but has recorded and performed with greats like Jimmy Buffett, Roy Orbison, George Jones, Chet Atkins, Dolly Parton, Greg "Fingers" Taylor, Tammy Wynette, The Osmond Brothers, Jerry Lee Lewis, Mickey Gilley, Ray Stevens, Charley Pride, and many others.

He wrote commercials and jingles for Maybelline Cosmetics, STP, Coors Beer, and Mercury Outboard Engines. He has also recorded soundtracks on electric bass for four Clint Eastwood movies including *Every Which Way But Loose* and *Thunderbolt and Lightfoot*. Other movies include *Smokey and the Bandit* with Burt Reynolds and *Honeymoon in Vegas* with Nicolas Cage.

Johnson has performed on more than thirty TV shows, including "The Tonight Show," "The Music City Awards," "Jerry Lewis MD Telethon," "Bob Hope Special," "The Merv Griffin Show," "Nashville on the Road," "Starsky and Hutch," "Barbie Benton Special," "American Bandstand," and "The Joan Rivers Show."

Johnson describes himself as a behind-the-scenes kind of guy but his talent has taken him where most will never walk.

Fred Knobloch is a country singer and songwriter born in Jackson on April 28, 1953. His hit records include *Why Not Me* (No. 18 in 1980), which he wrote, and *Killin' Time* (No. 28 in 1981), a duet with TV/film actress Susan Anton. He had a No. 1 country single with the group Schuyler, Knobloch & Overstreet, *Baby's Got a New Baby*, in 1986. He co-wrote the B. J. Thomas hit, *The Whole World's In Love When You're Lonely.*

Leake County Revelers. String bands performed a style of country music called old-time country. These bands were noted for their emphasis on instrumental formation rather than singers. They were popular during the 1920s, and the Leake County Revelers may be the best example of what became known as Mississippi string bands. The band was discovered by famed talent scout H. C. Speir.

The Leake County Revelers were led by fiddler Will Gilmer, born in 1895 in Sebastopol. Indeed, the band was from Sebastopol in Scott County and not from Leake County. The band's other members were R. O. Mosley on banjo-mandolin, Jim Wolverton on banjo, and Dallas Jones on guitar and lead vocals.

The band played hoe-downs, rags, pop songs, parodies, waltzes, and sang barbershop quartet style. Some say it was a show band and it did experiment with different sounds.

The group's playing is representative of

Leake County Revelers (left to right) Dallas Jones, R. O. Mosley, Jim Wolverton, and Will Gilmer.

Mississippi's smooth sound, due primarily to the gliding fiddle playing of Gilmer. His relaxed bowing emphasizes smooth notes rather than a choppy delivery. His constant slides in pitch, coupled with the usual Mississippi practice of tuning the fiddle below standard pitch, marked him as an excellent practitioner of what developed as the Mississippi string band style.

Gilmore, like other Mississippi fiddlers, usually streamlined the melody of fast dance tunes. The band also tended to play tunes slower than did their counterparts in the southeastern mountains.

The band recorded such songs as *Mississippi Moon Waltz, Picture No Artist Can Paint, Lazy Kate, Dry Town Blues, Georgia Camp Meeting,* and *Leake County Blues. Mississippi Moon Waltz* was one of the best-selling country records in the 1920s.

The Leake County Revelers recorded forty-four songs for Columbia between 1927 and 1930, and were one of the best selling groups of the period.

The group broke up in the early 1930s.

Chris LeDoux was born on October 2, 1948, in Biloxi. When LeDoux was growing up, his family lived in several states, mainly Texas. He won a world rodeo championship title in bareback bronc riding. All the while, he was writing music about the things he knew—his cowboy's life. He was called the "Singing Bronc Rider."

He recorded his own songs in 1972 and sold the tapes out of the back of his old pick-up truck along the rodeo circuit.

Chris LeDoux

Between 1973 and 1991 he released such albums as *Wild and Wooly, Rodeo Songs,* and *Old Cowboy Heroes.* Liberty Records signed him to a contract and he toured to promote *The Best of Chris LeDoux,* a compilation album, which Liberty released in 1992.

He has twenty-six albums and was nominated for a Grammy in 1993 for Best Country Vocal Collaboration with Garth Brooks for the song *Whatcha Gonna Do With A Cowboy.* It reached the gold record level. LeDoux is known for his releases *Haywire, The Best of Chris LeDoux,* and home video *Chris LeDoux Live.*

Mac McAnally was born in Red Bay, Alabama, on July 1, 1957, but grew up in Belmont. He is known for his songwriting and guitar playing, but he started out playing the piano. His mother taught

69 • COUNTRY

him how to play and the young McAnally played in church.

He began recording in Muscle Shoals, Alabama; his debut, *It's A Crazy World,* went to No. 2 on the charts and broke over into pop's Top 40 in 1977. He was only eighteen years old at the time and was already an established singer and songwriter.

McAnally is known for such tunes as *Old Flame* by Alabama, *Two Dozen Roses* by Shenandoah; *Thank God For You* and *All These Years* by Sawyer Brown; and *It's My Job* by Jimmy Buffett. McAnally was signed by Dreamworks Records in Nashville in 1998.

Elsie McWilliams was born in Meridian on June 1, 1896. She had a large role in shaping Jimmie Rodgers' career. She was his sister-in-law and wrote thirty-nine songs for him, although she is credited with only nineteen. She also used her song writing ability for Ernest Tubb.

McWilliams was inspired to write such tunes as *My Old Pal, My Little Old Home Down in New Orleans, Daddy and Home,* and *Lullaby Yodel.* Jimmie Rodgers often said that McWilliams was his greatest musical inspiration because the words she wrote made him want to sing.

On October 7, 1979, she was inducted into the Songwriters Hall of Fame in Nashville. She is often referred to as the "Grandma Moses of Country Music Writing." McWilliams continued living a simple life despite her successes. She lived in Meridian most of her life and died there December 30, 1986, at the age of ninety.

McWilliams was recently inducted into the Mississippi Musicians Hall of Fame.

Paul Overstreet was born March 1, 1955. He is a native of Vancleave and left for Nashville after graduating from high school. He played bass, drums, and guitar on the road with different bands. In 1985 he returned to Nashville from the road and began to concentrate on his song writing.

By 1987, Overstreet had received the Nashville Songwriters Association International Songwriter of the Year. He also received BMI's Songwriter of the Year honors in 1987 and 1988.

He co-wrote Randy Travis' song *On the Other Hand,* which was voted Song of the Year in 1987 by the Country Music Association and the Academy of Country

Paul Overstreet

Music. He teamed with co-writer Don Schlitz again in 1988 for Travis' *Forever and Ever Amen*. It won a Grammy Award and became TNN's Viewer's Choice Awards Favorite Song in 1988.

His songwriting efforts produced The Judds' Grammy Award Winner, *Love Can Build A Bridge*. The song was co-written with Naomi Judd and John Jarvis.

Overstreet earned BMI's Songwriter of the Year from 1987 until 1992. He had such hits as *Sowin' Love, All the Fun, Seein' My Father In Me, Richest Man on Earth,* and *Love Helps Those.*

In June 1990, Overstreet was named Mississippian of the Year by the Mississippi Broadcasters Association. The same year, he was named National Spokesperson for Project Literacy for the anthem *Billy Can't Read*. RCA turned this inspiring song into a music video and it has been distributed to many state literacy programs.

In 1994, Overstreet was voted the TNN/Music City News Christian Country Artist of the Year.

Ben Peters was born on January 20, 1937, in Hollandale. He started playing in bands when he was only fourteen years old and after he graduated from the University of Southern Mississippi, served four years in the Navy. In 1966, Peters left Mississippi to go to Nashville, the country music capital of the world.

Eddy Arnold recorded Peters' *Turn the World Around* and made it No. 1. In 1970, Peters started his own production company, Ben Peters Music. In 1972, he won the Grammy Award for *Kiss An Angel Good Morning*.

By 1973, he had earned Best Male Country Writer by *Billboard* magazine. Then in 1975, Peters was named Songwriter of the Year by the Nashville Songwriters Association and was inducted into the Nashville Association International Hall of Fame in 1980.

His song, *Before the Next Teardrop Falls,* was Music Operators of America's Record of the Year in *Juke Box* and *Record World* magazines. He has written more than 1,000 songs that are known in the United States and Europe. Such songs are, *Daytime Friends* sung by Kenny Rogers, *Tell Me What It's Like* sung by Brenda Lee, *Burger and Fries* sung by Charley Pride, and *Before My Time* sung by John Conlee. He has enjoyed international successes with *Everything to Me* and *I Want To Wake Up With You*. Both of these songs were No. 1 hits in England and eventually in Australia.

Peters' songs have been played on radio more than thirteen million times and some of his songs have been in the movies. His songs have been recorded by more than 150 different artists in the United States and abroad.

Peters was recently inducted into the Mississippi Musicians Hall of Fame.

Clyde Pitts was born in Jackson and has been a music business professional for the past thirty years. He is known by many of the biggest names in country music as a singer, musician, lead guitarist, songwriter. Known specifically as

Clyde Pitts

a "songwriter" now, he has recorded for Columbia, Monument, Challenge, Everest, and other record companies during his career.

In 1959, he left Mississippi for California where he lived in Los Angeles and Hollywood until 1966. His first professional job was playing lead guitar with Wynn Stewart at a well-known Long Beach, California, nightclub, George's Round-Up. There he met and became close friends with steel guitarist, Ralph Mooney (now world-famous and a member of Waylon Jennings' band).

After a few months at George's Round-Up, Pitts formed his own band and worked various clubs in Los Angeles, as well as Las Vegas, with some well-known West Coast artists. In 1962, he settled down to one club, The Foot Hill Club, for the next four years.

Pitts' first song recorded on a major label (RCA) was *Almost Alone* performed by Gordon Terry in June 1960. During the early 1960s, he had several songs recorded by artists such as Rosemary Clooney, Tab Hunter, Lou Rawls, Ricky Nelson, Carl Belew, Carl Smith, Roy Drusky, Jerry Wallace, Gene Vincent, Ray Pillow, Dottie West, Jeannie Seeley, Glen Campbell, Bobby Bare, and other well-known artists.

Quite a number of songs were written during the next few years by Pitts and his close friend Carl Belew such as *Even The Bad Times Are Good,* considered a standard song in the business today. The song was recorded by many artists such as Jerry Wallace, Faron Young, George Jones, Tammy Wynette, Bobby Bare, Nat Stuckey, Connie Smith, The London Philharmonic Orchestra, and many others. Other songs written or co-written by Pitts have been hits and in the national charts such as *Sweetheart of The Year* and *Happy Anniversary* performed by Ray Price (a Top 10 hit in 1969); *Sad Situation* performed by Skeeter Davis and later by Tracy Nelson.

In addition to artists already mentioned, he has had songs recorded by Conway Twitty, Charley Pride, Jerry Lee Lewis, Charley Walker, Jody Miller, Eddy Arnold, and Slim Whitman.

Pitts now lives in Jackson.

Charley Pride was born March 18, 1938, in Sledge. His family were sharecroppers and Pride got his first taste of music listening to the Grand Ole Opry on radio. He bought his first guitar at age fourteen and taught himself to play. He learned by imitating the sounds he heard on the radio.

In 1954, Pride entered his first musical talent contest at Lowe's Grand Theater in Memphis, Tennessee. He was chosen as a semifinalist but his other love, baseball, took him away from music. He divided his time between the two interests.

In 1965, Chet Atkins of RCA in Nashville signed Pride and his first single, *The Snakes Crawl at Night,* was released. It was followed by *Just Between You and Me* and many other hits. *Just Between You and Me* won the Grammy nomination in 1966 for Best Country and Western Male Vocal Performance. Pride won three Grammy Awards between 1965 and 1975 and of twenty-two albums, twelve went gold.

Pride made his first appearance at the Grand Ole Opry in January 1967. He was the first black superstar to be rec-

> •••••
> ## Mississippi First:
> CHARLEY PRIDE, BORN IN SLEDGE, WAS THE FIRST AFRICAN-AMERICAN TO BE INDUCTED INTO THE GRAND OLE OPRY.
> •••••

ognized by the country music scene. He is known for such hits as *Does My Ring Hurt Your Finger, I Know One, I Can't Believe You Stopped Loving Me, Let The Chips Fall, I'd Rather Love You, Let Me Live,* and *Kiss an Angel Good Morning.*

Pride has won Artist of the Year and Best Male Country Vocalist of the Year from the Country Music Association. He won Music Operators of America's Top Country Artist and Top Male Vocalist (1971, 1972). *Cashbox Magazine* gave him Top Male Vocalist for Country Music.

Even more of his hits include *Mississippi Cotton Pickin' Delta Town, Is Anybody Goin' to San Antone?, When I Stop Leavin' I'll Be Gone,* and *Burgers and Fries.*

By 1984, Pride had thirty-six No. 1 hit songs. He also sold more than twenty-five million albums worldwide and holds thirty-one gold and four platinum

Charley Pride

LeAnn Rimes

albums, one of which is a quadruple-platinum.

On May 1, 1993, Pride was inducted into the Grand Ole Opry, the first African-American to receive this honor in the Opry's seventy-one years. He has also been recognized on the Hollywood Walk of Fame with a star.

In 1994, he released his autobiography, *Pride: The Charley Pride Story*. He owns a theater in Branson, Missouri, and currently resides in Dallas, Texas, where he deals in real estate and banking investments. Pride always remembers his roots. He says during shows, "I always ask my audiences for a round of applause for my hometown, Sledge, Mississippi. I love my home state."

Margaret LeAnn Rimes was born on August 28, 1982, in Jackson. Rimes won her first talent contest at the age of five and almost won the lead in Broadway's *Annie 2* at age six. At age six, she moved to Texas where she portrayed Tiny Tim in a local musical and at age eight, she was a two-week champion on TV's "Star Search." At age eleven, she recorded her first album, *All That*. After the success of her album, Rimes recorded another album titled *Unchained Melody:The Early Years*. The songs on this album were recorded when Rimes was only twelve; critics said that at fourteen, Rimes seemed experienced beyond her years. In May 1996, her yodel-filled recording of *Blue* hit the *Billboard* charts and was a huge radio success and a multi-platinum seller. It made her an instant star.

In 1996, she won awards such as the Academy of Country Music Single of the Year, the Academy of Country Music Song of the Year, Academy of Country Music Top New Female Vocalist, Grammy Best Female Country Vocal Performance, and Grammy Best New Artist.

In 1997, she won American Music Awards' Favorite New Artist, the CMA Horizon Award, and TNN/Music City News Stars of Tomorrow–Female. Her semi-autobiographical novel, *Holiday in Your Heart,* was published in 1997. In June 1998, she was again nominated as Best Female Artist by the TNN Music City News Country Awards. Her *How Do I Live* was a certified multi-platinum in 1998.

Her third CD, released in 1998, *You Light Up My Life: Inspirational Songs,* debuted at No.1 on three different *Billboard* charts. She can be seen regularly on Nashville TV.

James Charles "Jimmie" Rodgers was born in Meridian on September 8, 1897. He won his first musical prize at age twelve when he won a local amateur contest for singing *Billy Baily* and *Steamboat Bill.* His father was a section foreman on the Mobile and Ohio Railroad, now the Illinois Central Gulf. When he was fourteen, he was a full-fledged railroad brakeman. Rodgers often carried his guitar to work with him and entertained his co-workers, which earned him the nicknames, "Singing Brakeman" and "America's Blue Yodeler."

In 1924, Rodgers' health began to fail. He was admitted to the hospital with a very bad cough caused by tuberculosis, and his health didn't get better during the three months he stayed in bed. He left the hospital because he had to provide for his family, and started riding the rails. But the strain proved too much for his tuberculosis-ridden body and he was forced to return to the hospital.

The family moved to Asheville, North Carolina, and Rodgers formed his band, "Jimmie Rodgers and The Entertainers." He played anywhere he could earn a little money. His persistence paid off on August 4, 1927, when RCA Victor had a talent scout in the area and Rodgers went to audition. He played the lullaby, *Sleep, Baby, Sleep* and *The Soldier's Sweetheart* which led to his recording of the immortal *Blue Yodel,* Rodgers' first big hit.

One interesting and little-known fact is that Rodgers had tried out earlier for H. C. Speir in Jackson, a well-known talent scout for RCA Victor. When Speir

> **Mississippi First:**
> JIMMIE RODGERS, BORN IN MERIDIAN, WAS THE FIRST PERSON ELECTED TO THE COUNTRY MUSIC HALL OF FAME AND IS CONSIDERED TO BE THE "FATHER OF COUNTRY MUSIC."

heard Rodgers sing, he told him to go home to Meridian and practice.

Before and after his success, Rodgers played with black blues artists in Mississippi and elsewhere. He liked to sing the blues and this led to his creating his unique "country music" sound.

By the spring of 1928, Rodgers' records were selling. Within six months,

Jimmie Rodgers, the Father of Country Music.

he was earning $2,000 a month for doing what he loved, singing and playing the guitar, a considerable sum at the time. The Great Depression could not even touch him because by then, he was already a millionaire. Rodgers eventually moved the family into a mansion in Kerrville, Texas, but in 1930, his health was failing again.

On May 26, 1933, Rodgers died of the lung disease that had plagued him all his young life. Rodgers is buried in Oak Grove Cemetery in Meridian.

Rodgers is called the Father of Country Music and considered to be the man who started it all. He was the first country star inducted into the Country Music Hall of Fame in 1961. In only five years of a professional music career, he recorded sixty records that sold more than twenty million copies. Some of his classics include *Waiting for the Train, Daddy and Home, Frankie and Johnny, T. B. Blues, Miss the Mississippi and You,* and *My Blue-Eyed Jane.*

Jimmie Rodgers was recently inducted into the Mississippi Musicians Hall of Fame.

Jesse Otto Rodgers was born on March 5, 1911, a few miles from Waynesboro. Soon after Rodgers was born, his father Eff decided to give up farming and join his brother Aaron. Aaron was the father of the famous "Singing Brakeman" and "Blue Yodeler," Jimmie Rodgers, so Jesse Rodgers was the first cousin of Jimmie Rodgers. Aaron Rodgers was employed with the Illinois Central Railroad, and Jesse's father went to work for the same company.

During this period Jimmie and Jesse attended school together in the mornings, and in the afternoons, they worked on the farm. Jimmie taught Jesse his first two chords on the guitar. They would sit under a big oak tree at the edge of the field and pick and sing. While Jimmie guided the mule and plowed a couple of turns, Jesse would pick and sing and then plow while Jimmie picked and sang. This arrangement was the beginning of the legend of Jimmie and Jesse Rodgers. Together, these two country yodelers have recorded a total of 168 songs for RCA Victor.

Jesse began his professional career working for radio stations XEPN and XERA in Texas and in Mexico just across the border from Eagle Pass, Texas. He would do five shows a day, singing, playing, and announcing. His first show started at 5:00 a.m., and his last show ended at midnight.

During this time, a talent scout from RCA Victor Bluebird asked Jesse to record for them. Only one year earlier, Jimmie Rodgers had recorded his last song. In 1933, the nation mourned the death of Jimmie Rodgers. One of his final requests was that Jesse carry on the famous blue yodeling that Jimmie had introduced to the world. Jesse did this by recording *The Rambler's Yodel* and *Yodeling the Railroad Blues.*

From the time of his first recording on March 26, 1933, to his last on May 15, 1960, Jesse recorded seventy-two songs for RCA Victor. Some of his very first were recorded in Camden, New Jersey and San Antonio, Texas.

Some of his best-known recordings are *Blue Christmas, Here Comes Santa Claus, Within This Evil Heart, Sweeter Than The Flowers, Hadacol Boogie, Country Boy, Wedding Bells, Tennessee Polka, Why Don't You Haul Off And Love Me, Mind Your Own Business, Cry Baby Heart,* and *I'll Go Chasing Women.*

He had radio programs in Dallas, Kansas City, Chicago, St. Louis, and Philadelphia, one of which was the national broadcast "Hayloft Hoedown." He starred, with his trained horse, in one of the first live television western shows called "Western Balladeer" on WPTZ. Following this was a filmed television series called "Ranger Joe," a CBS television network program starring Rodgers as the typical sagebrush hero. Co-starring with Jesse on the "Ranger Joe" program was his educated Palomino horse Topaz.

Rodgers died in December 1973 in Houston, Texas.

Johnny Russell was born in Roundaway in Sunflower County on January 23, 1940. His family moved to Fresno, California, when he was twelve. He became very active singing and writing music and worked as a disc jockey on KEAP radio. He began performing in clubs around town and writing songs. He wrote and recorded his first hit, *In a Mansion Stands My Love,* when he was only eighteen.

Russell moved to Nashville, where Jim Reeves recorded Russell's *In a Mansion Stands My Love* and on the flip side, *He'll Have to Go.* While in Nashville, Buck Owens recorded Russell's *Act Naturally* in 1963. The song sold more than twenty million copies internationally and was also recorded by Ringo Starr of The Beatles in 1989.

Russell wrote songs for Dolly Parton, Emmylou Harris, and Linda Ronstadt. He has also wrote *Let's Fall To Pieces Together* for George Strait; *You'll Be Back* for The Statler Brothers; *Got No Reason for Goin Home* for Gene Watson; and *The Only Fire That Burns* for Bobby Vinton. He has also written songs for Loretta Lynn, Burl Ives, Dottie West, Patti Page, and countless others.

His own hits include *Mr. and Mrs. Untrue, Rain Falling on Me, Rednecks, Catfish John, Hello I Love You,* and *Song of the South.*

He became a member of the Grand Ole Opry in 1985 and began appearing as a regular performer on "Hee Haw." Russell was nominated for a Grammy Award as Male Vocalist of the Year in 1973 and received awards from BMI Achievement and RCA Records' Golden Boot Award. Mississippi Governor Ray Mabus proclaimed May 19, 1988, as "Country Music Day" in honor of Russell's outstanding talents and achievements. Mississippi Delta Community College designated the same day "Johnny Russell Day."

Bob Saxton was born in Newton County but lived in Jackson for nearly

Bob Saxton

twenty years. Early in his career, he played guitar with Patsy Cline, Bobbie Gentry and Jimmy and Tommy Dorsey. In the 1970s, he started playing in churches and prisons in and around Anchorage, Alaska.

In 1995, Saxton appeared in France at the World Guitar Festival. After moving to Nashville, he played at the Grand Ole Opry with Billy Walker. For nine months in 1984, he played the Opry with Charlie Lorvin.

Saxton was inducted into the New York Country Music Hall of Fame. He won the Merle Travis National Thumb Pickers Contest twice. He has also toured and recorded in Germany.

Lisa Stewart, a native of Louisville, was born on August 6, 1968. She began singing her favorite song, *Delta Dawn,* at age three. Stewart made her first solo appearance at church and soon other churches wanted the little performer to sing for them.

She sent a tape to Nashville's "Fan Fair" when she was eleven and was chosen to sing in the Fair's tent show. She also performed in local theaters, played in the school jazz band, and was a majorette. Stewart continued her music training by studying voice at Mississippi University for Women and later transferred to Belmont University in Nashville to accept a Roy Acuff Vocal Scholarship.

At Belmont University, Stewart was encouraged to focus on opera. She often did local commercial work for television. She signed with BNA and in May of 1994, released *Solitary Heart.*

The release of *Solitary Heart* marked her exit from the cast of "Music City Tonight," so she could devote all her efforts to touring. She is known for songs such as *Let's Go To Vegas, Hold Me, Love Without Mercy,* and *Fall For Me Again.* Her more recent releases include an album, *Lisa Stewart,* and a single, *Drive Time.* She has had hits in Europe as well as the United States.

Marty Stuart was born September 30, 1958, and is a native of Philadelphia. He started singing professionally when he was eleven years old. He was part of the gospel tent group The Sullivans. At twelve he went on the road with Lester Flatt's bluegrass band. By the time he was thirteen, he had made his first appearance at the Grand Ole Opry.

Lester Flatt died in 1979 and Stuart started touring with Johnny Cash. Stuart continued to play in country music until 1982 when his first solo album, *Busy Bee Cafe,* was released on the independent Sugar Hill label.

Marty Stuart

In 1986, his first major label debut was *Marty Stuart* on CBS Records. His first big success came in 1990 with *Hillbilly Rock,* released on MCA and that hit was followed with *Tempted.*

In 1990, Stuart joined with country music star Travis Tritt for their popular No Hats Tour. *This One's Gonna Hurt You* became Marty's first gold album.

In 1992, Stuart was inducted into the Grand Ole Opry. In the same year, he won a Grammy Award and was inducted into the Country Music Hall of Fame's Walkway of Stars. He won the Country Music Association's Award for Vocal Events for his teaming with Travis Tritt. Also in 1992, he released his anthology, *The Marty Party Hit Pack.*

One of his latest CDs is *Pilgrim,* and he has written a photo-packed book of short stories entitled *Pilgrims: Sinners, Saints and Prophets.* He has written scores for Billy Bob Thornton's movies *Daddy and Them* and *All the Pretty Horses,* and Martin Scorcese's *Hi-Lo Country.*

In 1997, the Discovery Channel Online featured a ten-day cross country tour documenting Stuart's day-to-day activities. In his career, he has been nominated for eight Grammy Awards and has won three.

It would be a mistake to classify Stuart as a country singer only. His talents include singer, guitarist, poet, author, TV host, producer, actor, soundtrack composer, photographer, and songwriter.

On July 8, 1997, Stuart married Connie Smith.

"Conway Twitty" or Harold Lloyd Jenkins, was born September 1, 1933, in Friars Point. His father, a ferryboat captain, was a musician and his grandfather gave the young Jenkins a ukulele on which he taught himself to play.

His first band was formed when he was only ten years old. At age twelve, he

•••••
Mississippi First:

CONWAY TWITTY, BORN IN FRIARS POINT, WAS FIRST IN NO. 1 HIT RECORDS. HE HAD OVER 50 NO. 1 HITS—MORE THAN ANY OTHER ARTIST IN ANY GENRE, INCLUDING ELVIS AND THE BEATLES.

•••••

formed the Phillips Country Ramblers and performed on KFFA radio in Helena, Arkansas.

He was offered a position by the Philadelphia Phillies baseball team when he graduated high school. He did not accept the offer.

Jenkins was drafted into the Army during the Korean War, and was stationed in Japan where he formed The Cimmarons and entertained the troops. When Jenkins returned home, rock and roll had become popular. He had planned on pursuing his baseball career until he heard Elvis Presley sing. He tried to imitate Presley but was not successful.

He changed his name in 1957 to Conway Twitty. The "Conway" comes from Conway, Arkansas, and the "Twitty" from Twitty, Texas.

The newly named Conway Twitty recorded three singles that year for Mercury Records. They were somewhat successful and *I Need Your Loving* made the *Billboard* charts. He continued to play in honky-tonks around Arkansas. He changed labels and went with MGM on a five-year contract. The songs *It's Only Make Believe* and *I'll Try* were recorded during this early period.

Conway Twitty

It's Only Make Believe proved to be the hit that made Twitty (Jenkins) a star. It was No. 1 and in 1959, Twitty went on a European tour. There his popularity was second only to Elvis.

Upon his return to the United States, he appeared in several motion pictures such as *College Confidential, Platinum High School* and *Sex Kitten Goes to College*.

By 1960, Twitty had a hit with *Lonely Blue Boy* and returned to England to tour. For the next two years, his records continued to produce hits like *Portrait of a Fool*.

In 1963, he signed with ABC-Paramount where *Walk Me to the Door* achieved moderate success. In 1965, Twitty switched to Decca Records and his second recording, *The Image of Me,* made the country charts Top 10.

In 1969, Twitty began singing duets with Loretta Lynn. They recorded five No. 1 hits and won Country Music Association's Vocal Duo of the Year for four consecutive years, 1972 to 1975. They received the coveted Grammy Award in 1971 for their duet, *After the Fire Is Gone.* Twitty ended up with more than fifty No. 1 hits, twenty of which he wrote himself.

Twitty City Park in Nashville opened in 1981 and by this time, Twitty's success was almost immeasurable. He had more than 200 published songs and more No. 1 records than Elvis Presley, Johnny Cash, The Beatles or any other artist in history. Conway Twitty died on June 5, 1994, at the age of fifty-nine.

Tammy Wynette was born in Tremont in Itawamba County on May 5, 1942, as Virginia Wynette Pugh. She was reared by her grandparents in Mississippi and Alabama and grew up singing with her musical family. She worked many hours in the cotton fields in Itawamba County.

In the 1950s, she performed on local gospel radio with a group called "Wynette, Linda and Imogene." In 1961, Wynette married a month before her high school graduation. She had a daughter the same year and another one the following year.

In 1965, after having her third daughter, Wynette divorced her husband. She enrolled in cosmetology school and took her family to Birmingham, Alabama, where she worked as a beautician. She never abandoned music and sang on a morning television show while in Birmingham.

In 1966, Wynette decided to go to Nashville. With help from producer Billy Sherrill, she made her first record, *Apartment #9,* written by Johnny Paycheck.

In 1967, she followed that release with *Your Good Girl's Gonna Go Bad,* which became her first No. 1 hit. That year she also won a Grammy Award for *I Don't Wanna Play House.* Then in 1969, her famous hit, *Stand By Your Man,* moved

> **Mississippi First:**
> TAMMY WYNETTE, BORN IN TREMONT, WAS THE FIRST FEMALE COUNTRY ARTIST TO HAVE A MILLION-SELLING ALBUM. THAT EARNED HER THE NAME "FIRST LADY OF COUNTRY MUSIC."

from country music charts into pop and won her another Grammy.

That same year, she was named Country Music Association's Female Vocalist of the Year and the Academy of Country Music's Top Female Vocalist. She was again CMA's Female Vocalist of the Year in 1970.

Tammy Wynette, First Lady of Country Music.

In 1969, Wynette and George Jones married and began recording duets in 1971. *Till I Get it Right, Golden Ring,* and *Near You* were all No. 1 hits. Although they divorced in 1975, they still sang together years later.

She worked with stars like Burt Reynolds and Randy Travis. She won every award that country music has to offer and she holds two Grammys, sixteen BMI song writing honors, and three Country Music Association awards.

Her life story was a hit television movie and her famous *Stand By Your Man* was a hit in eighteen countries worldwide. More than thirty million copies of Wynette's records were sold. Because she was the first female country artist to have a million-selling album, she was named the "First Lady of Country Music." Wynette died on April 6, 1998, of a blood clot at age fifty-five.

Wynette was recently inducted into the Mississippi Musicians Hall of Fame.

Gospel and Religious Music

.....

Gospel and other types of religious music have always had a strong role in Mississippi life. African-Americans combined European and African influences to create their own unique style of gospel. Small groups came out of Mississippi to tour the world. Recently it has taken on an almost jazz quality in large choirs. Highly emotional and repetitive musical themes dominate the music.

    White or southern gospel has had an effect on religious music throughout the world. In contrast to black gospel, southern gospel groups were mostly limited to small ensembles of four or five singers.

    Both black and white gospel music have had a profound effect on popular music. For example, Elvis Presley was greatly influenced by the Blackwood Brothers.

    In addition, Mississippians have had a great influence in performing and composing many other forms of religious and church music.

James Blackwood and the **Blackwood Brothers** were organized in Ackerman in 1934 with Roy, James, R. W., and Doyle Blackwood.

James Blackwood, the longest survivor of the original Blackwood Brothers Quartet, has been singing gospel music for more than sixty-six years.

> •••••
> ## Mississippi First:
> JAMES BLACKWOOD OF ACKERMAN IS THE FIRST AND ONLY PERSON IN ANY FIELD OF MUSIC TO HAVE BEEN NOMINATED FOR THE COVETED GRAMMY AWARD FOR 28 CONSECUTIVE YEARS.
> •••••

James Blackwood was born in Choctaw County. Together with his brothers, he formed a singing group that became world-famous. After singing with the Blackwood Brothers group for forty-seven years, he, together with four other well-known gospel singers from The Masters V, formed The James Blackwood Quartet in 1990.

During his long career, James Blackwood has been honored with more awards than any other gospel singer. He is the only person in any field of music to have been nominated for the coveted Grammy Award for twenty-eight consecutive years, and he has won nine Grammy Awards.

Peers in the Gospel Music Association voted him the Top Male Vocalist in Gospel Music for seven consecutive years. He was also the third living person to be voted into the Gospel Music Hall of Fame. He was inducted into the Southern Gospel Music Hall of Fame and the Mississippi Musicians Hall of Fame.

In 1983, Golden State University bestowed an honorary Doctoral Degree of Music on Blackwood. In 1986, Memphis State University voted him their Distinguished Achievement Award in the field of communications and fine arts. In 1997, the Memphis and Shelby County Optimist Clubs named him Citizen of the Year. They presented him with plaques and citations from sixteen government and civic groups.

In 1994, *The Singing News* presented James Blackwood with the Marvin Norcross Award. In 1997, *Gospel Voice* magazine gave him the Living Legend award. These are among the highest awards in gospel music.

James Blackwood has sung in all fifty states and in thirty-five foreign countries. He has appeared on "Arthur Godfrey Talent Scouts" (CBS), "Dave Garroway" (NBC), "Johnny Cash Show" (ABC), "Tennessee Ernie Ford Show" (ABC), "Tom Snyder Show" (NBC), "Dinah Shore Show," "Mike Douglas Show," and "Hee Haw" (CBS).

James Blackwood appeared on "The 700 Club" as well as in some of the nation's most prestigious churches such as the First Baptist-Dallas, First Baptist-Atlanta, First Assembly-Ft. Myers, First

James Blackwood

The original Blackwood Brothers Quartet: Roy, James, R.W., and Doyle, c. 1936.

Assembly-Phoenix, and First Church of the Nazarene-Denver.

Roy Pauley said, "My personal choice for the 1940s as gospel music's greatest singer has to be James Blackwood for his wonderful quality and voice clarity." Pauley continued, "James Blackwood and Jake Hess are Gospel Music's two greatest singers of the 20th Century."

The Blackwood Brothers Quartet

was formed in Choctaw County, Mississippi, in 1934, comprised of three brothers and the eldest son of the senior brother. (Roy, Doyle, and James were brothers; R. W. was the oldest son of Roy.) They began their career singing in churches around Choctaw County, with their first radio appearance on WHEF in Kosciusko. Later, they moved to Jackson where they broadcasted daily on WJDX. In 1939, they moved to Shreveport, Louisiana, where they broadcasted twice daily on KWKH. In 1940, they relocated again to Shenandoah, Iowa, where they were on the air three times daily on WKMS.

The start of World War II saw the group move to San Diego, where they worked in defense plants, sang on weekends, and performed a weekly radio program on WKGO. Although part of the group served in the military, the group remained solid. At the end of the war, they returned to Shenandoah, where they stayed until they moved to Memphis, Tennessee, in 1950.

In 1951, RCA Victor signed the Blackwood Brothers Quartet to a contract, and they recorded there for twenty-one years. Their records have sold in the millions and have been distributed worldwide. In 1954 and again in 1956, they won the "Arthur Godfrey Talent Scout Show," and were the only group to win twice. Their appearance on this show gave them national recognition. Commercial success was finally theirs. Instead of taking buses to the shows, they could now afford private planes. Unfortunately, on June 29, 1954, after an appearance in Gulfport, Mississippi, the band boarded a plane bound for Clanton, Alabama. At the Clanton Airport the plane crashed, taking the lives of two members, R. W. Blackwood and Bill Lyles. Despite the great loss, James

Blackwood took charge and reorganized, and the group continues to perform.

The group campaigned with their cousin, J. P. Coleman, for the office of Governor of Mississippi in 1955. Coleman won and gave credit to the Blackwood Brothers Quartet. James Blackwood said, "My motto and sole desire is to be used of God."

The Canton Spirituals, founded in Canton, blends rock and soul in a way that has kept it popular the world over for more than fifty years.

The original group included the songwriter and singer, Harvey Watkins, Sr., who began to sing in the group at age fourteen. The other original members were Eddie Jackson, Theo Thompson, and Roscoe Lucious.

Lead singer, Harvey Watkins, Jr., has been singing and performing with the group since he was a young child. The Canton Spirituals has been under his direction since the death of Harvey Watkins, Sr. Watkins, Sr., until his death, was the only original member with the Canton Spirituals. Cornelius Dwayne Watkins, singer and guitarist, later joined the group and Watkins, Jr., is his uncle.

In July 1994, Watkins, Sr. received a Legend Award at the Mississippi Gospel Music Awards. During the same month, Second Street in Canton, Mississippi, was renamed Harvey Watkins, Sr. Street in his honor. The Canton Spirituals has received numerous awards for its dynamic and spiritual music. The group was honored with Concurrent Resolution 557 from the Mississippi Legislature during their February 1998 regular session. The resolution recognized the group for receiving two Stellar Awards at the 1997 Stellar Gospel Music Awards and for being the only gospel quartet in America to receive those honors.

The Canton Spirituals also received the 1998 Excellence Award for Quartet of the Year-Traditional and LP of the Year-Traditional. The Canton Spirituals also won Group/Duo of the Year and Traditional Group/Duo at the thirteenth annual Stellar Awards.

Their album *Live in Memphis I* received a Grammy nomination, and they appeared at the awards show in April 1994. *Live in Memphis I* was also the longest-running album on *Billboard's* Gospel Music Chart as of November 1994. They were a part of the Gloryland's Gospel Music Top 15 Quartet Albums. Other awards and accomplishments include numerous Stellar, GMWA, Excellence, Dove, Soul Train, Urban Network Awards, and several Grammy Award nominations. They recently signed with Verity Records in New York.

The Canton Spirituals' album *Living the Dream: Live in Washington, D.C.* was a big success and featured hits like *Clean Up, Glad I've Got Jesus, Hallelujah Square,* and *Get Up in Me Jesus.* Their newer release, *The Live Experience 1999,* has been called one of their greatest projects.

Five Blind Boys of Mississippi, led by Archie Brownlee, was among several groups organized to raise funds for the

Piney Woods Day School south of Jackson in the 1930s. Originally a quartet known dually as The Cotton Blossom Singers (when perfoming popular music) and The Jackson Harmoneers (gospel). They became a quintet in the 1940s and changed their name to the Five Blind Boys of Mississippi. Members were Archie Brownlee, Joseph Ford, Lawrence Abrams, Lloyd Woodard, and Percell Perkins. Members of the group were blind.

The group left Piney Woods in 1944 to travel and record. They became superstars when their single *Our Father,* was a Top 10 R&B hit in the 1950s. They played to packed houses throughout the South and in 1965, toured Europe in the first Spiritual and Gospel Festival. The group continued into the 1990s, though many original members were replaced.

Some have compared the group's importance in gospel and rhythm and blues to that of Mississippian Lester Young's contribution to jazz sax. They influenced musicians like Ray Charles.

Their albums include *Soon I'll Be Done* (1952), *The Great Lost Album* (1957), *I'll Go* (1960), and fifteen others.

The Jackson Southernaires have awards showing them to be one of the best gospel groups in the country. The five members are: Huey Williams; Roger Bryant, Jr.; Maurice Surrell; James Burks; and Luther Jennings. Jennings is the only remaining original member. Another member of this group, Franklin Williams, was founder of the Mississippi Mass Choir (see entry).

The Jackson Southernaires

In 1940, The Jackson Southernaires were organized by Frank Crisler in Jackson and they began performing around their hometown of Jackson. The Jackson Southernaires were the first gospel group to use bass, drums, keyboard, and guitar.

After signing their first recording contract with Duke/Peacock Records in 1963, their *Too Late* was one of the top recording albums on that label. Later, The Jackson Southernaires signed a contract with the ABC/Dunhill label, with *Save My Child* and *Look Around,* two of the top albums on this record label in 1972-75.

In 1975, The Jackson Southernaires signed a recording contract with Malaco Records. Every album released has reached high in the ratings. In 1989, they released an album, *On The Third Day,* one of their best.

The Jackson Southernaires had their

own radio show for more than forty years and hosted their own television show called "Gospel Unlimited" for five years during the 1970s. The group was nominated for a Stellar Award in 1985 and 1986 and finally won the award in 1989. They received a Grammy nomination for *Thank You Mama* in 1991.

The Jackson Southernaires are known for such gospel favorites as *Keep On Praying, Can't Make It By Myself, Miracle, He Keeps on Blessing Me,* and *On the Third Day.*

Mississippi Mass Choir / Frank Williams. The founding and formation of the Mississippi Mass Choir was begun in 1988 by Frank Williams, an executive in the gospel music division of Malaco Records.

On October 29, 1988, the choir recorded its first album and video at the Jackson Municipal Auditorium, *The Mississippi Mass Choir Live.* In 1989, *Billboard* magazine certified it as the No. 1 spiritual album in the country after only five weeks.

The choir received four Stellar Awards: Choir of the Year, Album of the Year, Best New Artist, and Best Gospel Video. They also received nominations in several categories for the 1989 Soul Train Music Awards and the Dove Awards.

On December 8, 1990, the Mississippi Mass Choir recorded their second live project, *God Gets The Glory,* at the Mississippi Coliseum. *I'm Yours, Lord,* recorded with Willie Neal Johnson, won a Stellar Award. In October 1991, this album debuted on the *Billboard* charts in the number sixteen position. By December, the magazine had certified it as the No. 1 gospel album in the country. *Live with the Mississippi Mass Choir* was recognized by *Billboard* as the 1991 Album of the Year and received four Stellar Award nominations, winning the award for Best Gospel Video.

In 1991, the choir received a Stellar Award for Traditional Choir of the Year and was also nominated for Album of the Year and Video of the Year. *Billboard Magazine* again named the choir Gospel Artists of the Year. *God Gets the Glory* was named the 1992 Gospel Record of the Year by the magazine.

The choir received the Best Sellers Award from the National Association of Record Merchandisers and the Innovation Award from the 3M Corporation. In January 1993, the choir recorded its live album *It Remains To Be Seen.* Yet again, the album was certified as the No. 1 gospel album in the country and maintained the No. 1 position for eleven months.

The choir received Album of the Year and Choir of the Year awards at the 1993 Stellar Awards. *Your Grace and Mercy* received the Song of the Year award at the 1993 Gospel Music Workshop of America's Excellence Awards.

It Remains To Be Seen features the last recorded performance of the choir's founder, Frank Williams, who died of heart disease on March 22, 1993. The choir received an award at the 1994 Soul Train Music Awards for Best Gospel Album for this project.

Mississippi Mass Choir

In 1997, the Mississippi Mass Choir released another album and went on tour. The choir continues to rack up awards. They even sang for Pope John Paul II in Rome.

The Mississippi Mass Choir has recently been inducted into the Mississippi Musicians Hall of Fame.

Franklin D. Williams, founder of the Mississippi Mass Choir, was born June 25, 1947, in Smithdale. He started singing with The Southern Gospel Singers when he was five years old. After singing several years with his father's group, he joined The Jackson Southernaires with his brother. Frank and the Southernaires joined Malaco Records in 1975.

James Lloyd "Jimmy" Owens was born December 9, 1930, in Clarksdale and raised in Jackson. He started trumpet at age eleven and played in bands of Bailey Junior High, Central High School, and Millsaps College, and for four years in the Jackson Symphony Orchestra. He then traveled full-time with the Don Regon Orchestra.

Owens was converted in 1950. The Navy took him to California, where he became music director in a large church and met and married Carol Webb. In the 1960s, he conducted a number of chamber orchestra concerts with members of the San Francisco Symphony and was an arranger for Disneyland and for Stan Kenton's Collegiate Neophonic Orchestra.

But his main calling was music for ministry, to which he has dedicated his life ever since.

Owens is one of the pioneers of contemporary Christian music. In the early 1950s, when church music consisted usually of organ, piano and choir, Owens began experimenting with pop orchestra and vocal stylings and modern harmony in church. As one of the first arranger-conductor-producers of Christian recordings, he worked with such diverse artists as Pat Boone, Andrae Crouch, George Beverly Shea, Barry McGuire, and the Second Chapter of Acts and helped change the perception of Christian music.

But it was as a composer that he began to come into prominence in the 1970s. His over 200 recorded songs, including thirteen musicals written with his wife Carol, have affected the church worldwide. The best known of these are the musicals *Come Together, If My People,* and *The Witness.* Their musical *Ants'hillvania* was nominated for both Grammy and Dove awards in the category Best Album for Children.

The Owens are founders of the School of Music Ministries International, which has conducted numerous extended seminars in Asia, Africa, England, Australia, and Eastern Europe, as well as in the U.S. They are the

Jimmy Owens

authors of *Words and Music,* a book on Christian songwriting, and have toured and taught in some two dozen countries.

Music and ministry run in the family. Their daughter, Jamie Owens Collins, is a Christian songwriter and recording artist, and their son Buddy is an executive with Maranatha Music and a frequent emcee and speaker at Promise Keepers events. The Owens live in southern California, near their two children and seven grandchildren. Jimmy Owens is also the brother of Pat Fordice, who was Mississippi's First Lady from 1992-2000.

The Pilgrim Jubilees, otherwise referred to as "The Jubes," are known for lively and exciting gospel music. They were founded in 1944 by Elgie Graham and Willie Johnson of Houston, Mississippi. In 1946, Theophilles Graham, Monroe Hatchett, and Leonard Brownlee became members of the group, remaining until 1950 when Elgie Graham relocated to Chicago, Illinois. The group experienced a reorganization in the early 1950s when Elgie Graham brought in Major Roberson, Kenneth Madden, and his brothers, Cleve and Clay Graham.

Elgie retired in 1955 but encouraged the group to continue without him. Kenneth Madden left The Jubes, and Ben Chandler joined the group. Their first recording was released on Mashboro Records. Major Roberson and Rufus Crume composed and recorded *Stretch Out.* They caught the attention of Dick Clark while performing on a program in Atlanta. Clark recommended to Peacock-

Songbird Records that they sign the group. The release of *Stretch Out* gained national recognition and the album went gold.

In 1979, The Jubes signed with Savoy Records and released *Keep On Climbing, Put on Your Shoes, Whensoever I Pray,* and *Put Your Trust in Jesus.* These albums spawned such hits as *Rich Man, Poor Man; I'm Happy with Jesus Alone; Whensoever I Pray; Put Your Trust in Jesus; I'm Glad You Looked My Way,* among others.

The Jubes signed with Malaco Records in Jackson in 1987. They immediately released *Gospel Roots,* which reached the Top 40 on the gospel charts. Following *Gospel Roots,* they released *Back to Basics, Family Affair,* and *I'm Getting Better All The Time.* All these albums went to the Top 25 on the Billboard charts. *Family Affair* was nominated for a Stellar Award in 1991.

Roebuck "Pops" Staples was born on December 28, 1915, in Winona and is the founder of The Staple Singers. "Pops" Staples' introduction to music was from traditional and inspirational church sources. He also heard the blues and started playing the guitar in his teens.

He is a songwriter and guitarist who has influenced pop, rock, R&B, blues, and especially gospel music. In the 1930s, Staples introduced the use of blues guitars in gospel music, and in the 1960s he upset traditionalists by successfully moving from gospel to other genres.

The Staple Singers, made up of family members, had million selling records in

The Staple Singers

the 1970s like *I'll Take You There* and *Let's Do It Again.* Other hits included *Respect Yourself, If You're Ready,* and *Touch A Hand, Make A Friend.*

In 1991, Staples began touring solo and in 1992, The Staple Singers toured Europe. Pops Staples has recorded two CDs for Pointblank in a career that has covered more than fifty years. As a solo artist and as leader of The Staple Singers, his music is a blend of melody and message. His *Father Father* album, a 1994 Grammy-winning release, was a high point in his career. *Father Father* includes *Why Am I Treated So Bad* and *Waiting For My Child.* The rest of The Staple Singers, daughters Mavis, Yvonne, and Cleotha, also sing on the title track. Mavis Staples joins her father on *Hope In A Hopeless World.*

Pops Staples has appeared in three films: *Wag the Dog, Three Stories,* and a video called *Pops Staples—Live in Concert.*

In 1999, Staples was awarded the Mississippi Arts and Letters Special Award for his contribution to music.

The patriarch of The Staple Singers died on December 19, 2000, in his home in Dolton, Illinois.

Utica Jubilee Singers from Utica. This group toured the world spreading the "swing" of spirituals and gospel. They were the first black gospel quartet to be featured on a national radio show on a regular basis.

The Williams Brothers were organized in 1960 by Leon "Pop" Williams who was the founder and father of the group. This family of gospel music singers consisted of Leonard, Melvin, and Frank.

The group first recorded in 1973 on the Songbird Label and enjoyed immediate success with *Jesus Will Fix It*. They went on to record eighteen Top 10 albums listed in *Billboard* and *Cashbox* magazines. These releases earned three No. 1 record hits and three Grammy Award nominations.

The Williams Brothers are known for such songs as *Jesus Will Never Say No, I Won't Let Go of My Faith, He'll Understand, Sweep Around Your Own Front Door, The Goat, I'm Just a Nobody, Cover Me, In a Very Big Way,* and *A Ship Like Mine*. They teamed up with Anita Baker for a Grammy Award winner, *Ain't No Need To Worry*.

By April of 1991, The Williams Brothers had formed their own record label, Blackberry Records. They were again pioneers in that the Blackberry label is the only Mississippi recording company operated completely by African-Americans. Their first release, *This Is Your Night,* was nominated for a Grammy Award in the category of Best Soul Gospel Album-Traditional and went to No. 4 on the *Billboard* charts.

In January 1995, their release *In This Place* was nominated for a Grammy Award and won the Stellar Award for Best Performance by a Group or Duo.

The Williams Brothers have appeared at events such as Gospel Music Workshop of America, Dove Awards, Kentucky's Gospel Festival, and New Orleans Jazz Festival. They have been seen on many television shows such as "Soul Train Awards," "Stellar Awards," "CBS News," and "Living The Dream: A Tribute to Dr. Martin Luther King, Jr."

They have also performed in Madison Square Garden, Radio City Music Hall, Apollo Theater, Disneyland, Grand Ole Opry, and Carnegie Hall. The Williams Brothers have been honored in their hometown of Smithdale by having a road named after them—"Williams Brothers Road."

The Williams Brothers' careers have spanned twenty-five years of songwriting, performing, and producing.

Jazz

Jazz is another unique form of American music that has its roots in the South. Slaves took up playing European-type instruments in the early 1800s. These plantation bands led to minstrel, funeral, jug, and juke bands. Blues and ragtime styles developed later and were the forerunners of jazz.

In the opinion of the great blues artist from Mississippi, B. B. King, "Blues is the same as jazz. Jazz grew out of the blues." And the blues was born in the Mississippi Delta.

Mose John Allison was born in Tippo on November 11, 1927. Allison started taking piano lessons at age five but could already play by ear. He played trumpet in the band and dance bands in high school. He started composing songs when he entertained at parties. He listened to "boogie-woogie" music and liked Pete Johnson, Louis Armstrong, and Nat "King" Cole, all of whom influenced his style.

Although his grandmother died when his father was only a small infant, Allison says that his musical talent came from her.

Allison enrolled at the University of Mississippi in 1945, majoring in chemical engineering for one year. He then joined the military in 1946 and served in the army for six months at Fort McClellan, Alabama. While in the army, he played for an army band in Colorado Springs in the non-commissioners' and officers' clubs.

When he returned to the University of Mississippi, he majored in economics. While attending the university, he joined a dance band as arranger, piano, and trumpet player. Allison later formed his own trio and based its style on the music of Nat "King" Cole, Louis Jordan, and Errol Garner.

He graduated from Louisiana State University in 1952 with a B.A. in English and philosophy. He and his family moved to New York in 1956, where he began working in nightclubs and refined his very unique style of jazz, which is somewhere between blues and swing.

Mose Allison

He worked with jazz masters Stan Getz, Gerry Mulligan, Al Cohn, and Zoot Sims and has toured worldwide. Allison played a show with The Rolling Stones on August 7, 1964. He has recorded more than twenty albums, including *Lessons in Living* (1983) and *Ever Since The World Ended* (1989), both nominated for Grammy Awards.

Allison is also a songwriter. He has written more than 150 songs, which have been sung by Van Morrison (who did a tribute album to Allison in October 1996), John Mayall, The Who, Johnny Winter, The Clash, Eric Clapton, Elvis Costello, and Bonnie Raitt. Allison has influenced rockers such as Pete Townshend, Ray Davies, and Bill Wyman of The Rolling Stones. Some of his songs include *Hello There, Universe, I Don't Worry About A Thing,* and *Parchman Farm.* He recorded widely on Atlantic and Prestige.

Al Cohn arranged his first recording date, which included Allison, Bobby Brookmeyer, Nick Stabulas, and Teddy Kotick in New York. He started recording with Prestige and then recorded for Columbia Records for three years. His longest recording relationship, however, was with Atlantic Records, where he stayed for a decade and a half.

His first album was named *Cotton Country Suite.* Later, influenced by the classical composer Bela Bartok, he changed the album's name to *A Back Country Suite.*

He signed with Elektra/Musician in 1981 and made two albums, *Middle Class White Boy* and *Lessons in Living.* In 1996, Allison did a song with Van Morrison and Georgie Fame that sold more than 200,000 copies. This success led him to Blue Note for four titles, including *Gimcracks and Gewgaws* in 1998.

Mississippi First:

FREDERIC LEE BECKETT, BORN IN NETTLETON, IS RECOGNIZED AS THE FIRST GREAT MODERN TROMBONIST.

Frederic Lee Beckett was born in Nettleton on January 23, 1917. He attended high school in Tupelo and played trombone from 1940-44 with Lionel Hampton's band. He also played with J. J. Johnson, who considered Beckett to have been the first great modern trombonist. He also played with Andy Kirk, Prince Stewart, Nat Towels, and Johnson's Crackerjacks. He died on January 30, 1946.

Steve Blailock was born July 9, 1944, and was raised in McComb. Over the past three decades, the guitarist has performed and recorded with some of the greatest artists in the international jazz and blues field. These artists include Lou Rawls, Betty Carter, Hank Crawford, Arnett Cobb, Eddie "Cleanhead" Vinson, Jimmy Smith, Willie Mae "Big Mama" Thornton, Dr. Michael White, Jimmy Weatherspoon, Al Hirt, Pete Fountain, Harry Connick, Jr., and many others. Blailock is considered by his fellow musicians and peers to be a consummate guitar player with a unique style and artistic command of the instrument that is mastered by few.

Blailock was greatly influenced by New Orleans jazz and rhythm and blues, as well as the rich blues of his native Delta region. He was first introduced to music by his mother, who played piano and had a deep love and appreciation for jazz. Blailock moved to Nashville to study with the legendary guitarist Hank Garland. He found employment as a studio guitarist in the thriving Nashville

Steve Blailock

recording studios, where he remained for four years.

After moving to Los Angeles, this versatile guitarist was hired by Lou Rawls and became a fixture in the club scene.

Years of serious study with masters Joe Pass, Barney Kessel, Johnny Smith, Ellis Marsalis, and Herb Ellis did much to further improve Steve's understanding of jazz and the guitar.

In 1984, Blailock returned home to New Orleans. His credits include international tours from 1992 to 1995 with Greg Stafford, Dr. Michael White, and Lillian Boutte, as well as a 1995 tour of Scandinavia with his own band Swing Thing. He also teaches blues and jazz guitar in the Department of Jazz Studies at Dillard University, New Orleans, Louisiana. Since 1985, Blailock has appeared regularly with different bands at the Jazz and Heritage Festival New Orleans. He also performs with the famous Preservation Hall Jazz Band (banjo) and the Dukes of Dixieland in New Orleans

Recently he traveled to China to teach and perform at China's Jazz Festival.

Andrew "Andy" Blakney was born in Quitman on June 10, 1898. He played trumpet, recording with many legends of jazz, including King Oliver, Les Hite, Charles Echols, and with his own band. He joined Barry Martyn's Legends of Jazz and toured Europe.

Bobby Lee Bradford was born on January 19, 1934, in Cleveland. He was a trumpet player who emerged as one of the best from the avant-garde jazz scene. He grew up in Dallas where he played with local groups like Cedar Walton and David Newman. In 1953, he moved to Los Angeles where he played with Ornette Coleman and Eric Dolphy. Bradford spent time in the military and after, joined the Ornette Coleman Quartet in 1961 to 1963.

Bradford recorded with Ornette Coleman in 1971 but is also known for playing and recording with John Carter. He led his own quintet, the Mo'tet, which featured Vinny Golia. Bradford has worked with many jazz artists such as Fred Hopkins, David Murry, and Don Preston. He recorded with the Flying Dutchman, Revelation, and Enanem labels.

Richard Jess Brown was born in Jackson in 1956. He received his undergraduate degree in music education from Memphis State University and his master's in music performance from DePaul University. He has performed with many great classical and jazz artists such as Ella Fitzgerald, Pearl Bailey, Andre Watts, Lester Bowie, Ed Wilderson, and others. He has played on Top 10 albums and received international recognition, performing extensively in Europe. Articles about him and his music have appeared in *Newsweek, Downbeat, Coda,* and *Atlantic Monthly.*

Bobby Bryant was born in Hattiesburg in 1934. He played trumpet and tenor sax as a teenager, then moved to Chicago and studied music at the Cosmopolitan School of Music in 1957.

He played in Latin combos, small groups, and with Red Saunders. From 1960 to 1964, he traveled as lead trumpet player for Vic Damone in the U.S., Canada, and the Philippines. He was on the NBC-TV staff in New York and had his own combo. He worked with Peggy Lee, Lou Rawls, and Benny Goodman. He led the band on Bill Cosby's TV comedy series and other TV series. He recorded on Cadet and Vee-Jay labels.

His albums include *Big Band Blues* in 1961, *Earth Dance* in 1969, and *Swahili Strut* in 1971. However, he performed on hundreds of albums with other artists.

In addition to having his own group, he traveled with such big bands as Charlie Mingus, Oliver Nelson, Gerald Wilson, the Frank Capp/Nat Pierce Juggernaut, and the Clayton-Hamilton Jazz Orchestra.

Bobby Bryant died in June of 1998.

Delta Rhythm Boys was a jazz and vocal group founded by Lee Gaines of Buena Vista in the 1930s. They performed for more than fifty years and recorded with Count Basie and Ella Fitzgerald. The Delta Rhythm Boys were the first black entertainers to perform in Las Vegas. They had one hit, *Just A-Sittin' and A-Rockin',* in 1936. Their albums include *The Delta Rhythm Boys* on Mercury in 1952, *Dry Bones* on RCA in 1953, and *Singin' Spirituals* on Coral in 1961. They also appeared in more than thirty feature and musical films.

> • • • • •
> **Mississippi First:**
> THE DELTA RHYTHM BOYS FROM MISSISSIPPI WERE THE FIRST AFRICAN-AMERICAN ENTERTAINERS TO PERFORM IN LAS VEGAS.
> • • • • •

Theodore "Teddy"/"Babe Ruth" Edwards was born in Jackson on April 26, 1924. He played his first professional job at age twelve on the alto saxophone. He moved to Detroit and then to Los Angeles in 1944. He became known as an outstanding innovator of bebop and a brilliant improviser.

He switched from alto to tenor sax when he worked with Howard McGhee in the 1940s. He has performed in Europe and Japan and appeared with such greats as Hank Jones, Wardell Gray, Ernie Fields, Roy Milton, Charlie Parker, Dexter Gordon, Benny Carter, Red Callender, Gerald Wilson, and the Max Roach-Clifford Brown Quintet.

His records include *Around the Clock* with Wyonnie Harris and *Up in Dodo's Room* with Howard McGhee. He has been a band leader since 1958 and has also written film and soundtracks. He recorded on Onyx, Contemporary, Muse, Capitol, Verve, and Impulse labels.

His albums include *Teddy's Ready* in 1960 on the Original Jazz label, *Good Gravy* in 1981 on the Timeless label, and *Close Encounters* in 1999 on the High Note label.

Alvin Feilder was born in Meridian on November 23, 1935. He plays drums and does studio work for Duke Records. He also played with the Eddie Vinson Sextet. He has recorded for Delmark and now lives in Jackson.

John E. Gilmore was born September 28, 1931, in Summit. For most of his career he played tenor sax with one group, Sun Ra. His decision to play almost exclusively with Sun Ra long frustrated his jazz fans who felt that he could have made a bigger impact if he had developed a solo career.

Gilmore grew up in Chicago and after a stint in the Army (1948-52), he worked with Earl Hines (1952). In 1953, he joined Sun Ra and forty years later Gilmore was still there. His playing in the 1950s was an influence on the great John Coltrane.

Gilmore, who teamed up with Clifford Jordan for a 1957 Blue Note session, did spend 1964-65 with Art Blakey's Jazz Messengers. However, other than a few sideman recordings in the 1960s (including with Freddie Hubbard, McCoy Tyner, Andrew Hill, and Pete LaRoca), Gilmore stuck with Ra, being well-featured both on hard bop and free-form jazz. He briefly headed the Sun Ra group after Ra's death.

Gilmore worked with Jerry Gordon, Clifford Jarvis, Eloe Omoe, Robert Cummings, Michael Ray, Tyrone Hill, Robert Barry, Julian Priester, Walter Miller, Freddie Hubbard, Ali Hassan, James Jackson, Teddy Nance, and Lex Humphries. He was featured on tenor sax on many recordings, including a 1970 release by Futura, *Dizzy Reece/John Gilmore*.

He died on August 20, 1995, in Philadelphia, Pennsylvania.

James Richard "Dick" Griffin was born in Jackson where he studied trombone and piano at an early age. Griffin graduated from Jackson State University and received his master's degree from Indiana University. He taught school before going to New York to make his recording debut. He has recorded with Ella Fitzgerald, Duke Ellington, Marvin Gaye, Lou Rawls, and The Jacksons. He played for many Broadway productions, including *The Wiz, Black and Blue,* and *Lena.* His composition *World Vibration Suite* was premiered by the Brooklyn Philharmonic. His albums on Konnex Records include *Dream for Rahsaan* (1995), *Eight Wonders* (1995), and *All Blues* (1999).

Dardanelle Hadley was born around 1920 on a plantation in Avalon near Greenwood. She was encouraged to play the piano by her father, who liked Scott Joplin. Her father's sister was a concert pianist.

Hadley went to Louisiana State University on a bassoon scholarship. While there, she worked as a staff pianist on the Baton Rouge radio station WJBO. She had her own show and accompanied black singers.

She toured the country in the 1940s with her Dardanelle Trio. She cut her first recording with this group on RCA Victor and later for Columbia.

In the 1950s and 1960s, she worked on WGN Chicago TV as a staff member of a children's show. In the 1970s, she returned to the East Coast and resumed a career as a nightclub performer. She played all the major clubs in the Manhattan and Boston area, and appeared as a solo artist at Carnegie Recital Hall as part of the Newport/New York Jazz Festival.

As an internationally acclaimed jazz pianist, singer, and writer, Hadley made her mark in a man's world of jazz. She was listed in the *Jazz Journal International* which called her a "sophisticated jazz pianist with a pleasant singing voice." She was listed prominently in the book *Singing Jazz,* published by Miller-Freeman. The book tells the history of prominent female jazz singers in America.

Hadley never thought of herself as a singer, although she was cited as the up-and-coming female artist of the 1940s. Her talent as a singer and jazz piano player took her to Lincoln Center, Carnegie Hall, cruises on the *Queen Elizabeth II,* the Virgin Islands, London, Tokyo, and many other places in between.

John Wilson of the *New York Times* said, "She has an elastic rhythmic sense, and her improvisational turns enrich rather than distort her songs. She has a pure, gifted soprano [voice]. Singing is like breathing or sighing or walking to her, and song after perfect song rolls out."

Her albums include *Piano Mood Series* on Columbia in 1951, *Down Home* on Audiophile in 1985, *A Woman's Intuition* on Audiophile in 1992, *Swingin'* on Audiophile in 1994, and *Dardanelle Echoes Singing Ladies* in 1995 on Audiophile.

Hadley died in 1998 at her home in Winona where she had lived since 1996.

Michael Henderson was born in Yazoo City on July 7, 1951. At thirteen, Henderson played bass with the Fantastic Four, Detroit Emeralds, Billy Preston, and other Motown acts in 1964 and 1965. He later toured with Stevie

Wonder and Aretha Franklin before joining Miles Davis. He toured with Davis for seven years. Henderson made his vocal debut with Jean Carne singing *Valentine Love*. It reached No. 10 on the R&B charts and he then wrote two other hits, *We Both Need Each Other* and *You Are My Starship*. Recording for Buddah Records, Henderson got his first Top 10 recording, *Take Me I'm Yours,* in 1978. He earned his biggest hit in 1980 with *Wide Receiver* which made it to No. 4.

Two compilations of Henderson's work are *The Best of Michael Henderson* on the Sequel label in 1994 and *Best of Michael Henderson* on the Import label in 2000.

Arthur "Art" Hillery was born in New Orleans but grew up in Jackson. He began playing piano with local groups at an early age. He graduated from Jackson State University and has accompanied and recorded with a variety of big-name artists such as Ruth Brown, Joe Williams, Al Hibbler, and Ella Fitzgerald. He has performed in many countries, including Brazil, Japan, Norway, and Italy.

Hillery can be heard performing with Benny Carter, *My Kind of Trouble,* released in 1975; Teddy Edwards, *Mississippi Lad,* released in 1991; Ella Fitzgerald, *Incontournables,* released in 2000; and Milt Jackson, *Night Mist,* released in 1980.

Milt Hinton was born in Vicksburg on June 23, 1910. His family moved to Chicago in 1919. During his high school days, he played the fiddle and joined the marching band, where he played tuba. His first recording was made on tuba in 1930 with pianist Tiny Parham.

Hinton turned pro in high school and studied music at Crane Junior College and, for a short time, at Northwestern University. He recorded several sides and even sang on *Old Man Harlem* in 1933.

In 1936, Cab Calloway heard and saw Hinton in a Chicago jazz nightclub and hired him on the spot, a relationship that lasted fifteen years. With Cab Calloway, Hinton recorded what many consider to

> **Mississippi First:**
> MILT HINTON, BORN IN VICKSBURG, WAS THE FIRST BASS PLAYER TO BE FEATURED AS A SOLOIST ON A BIG BAND RECORDING, *PLUCKIN' THE BASS*. THAT RECORDING WAS WITH CAB CALLOWAY IN 1939.

be the first bass featured solo, *Pluckin' the Bass*. Other features came later with *Ebony Silhouette* and *Bassically Blue*. Hinton also played with Ben Webster, Chuck Berry, Dizzy Gillespie, and many others during that time.

Hinton joined the Louis Armstrong All Stars for several months that included a tour of Japan. When an offer came to join the CBS studio band, Hinton decided to leave Armstrong.

Hinton spent fifteen years in studios in

Milt "Judge" Hinton

New York. During that time, he performed with such notables as Johnny Mathis, Paul Anka, Bobby Rydell, Pearl Bailey, Bing Crosby, and Bobby Hackett; and he was helped by jazz lover Jackie Gleason.

He played bass and composed for some of the greats and served as studio musician with ABC and Dick Cavett. He toured the world with Barbra Streisand, Red Narvo, Teddy Gibbs, Bobby Hackett, and Pearl Bailey. He recorded on the Famous Door and Chiao labels.

Hinton was an avid photographer and has several books of great musicians he photographed over the years. He has assisted the National Endowment of the Arts in their Jazz Oral History Project and helped in other documentaries on jazz.

He was recently inducted into the Mississippi Musicians Hall of Fame. Called the "Judge," he is considered one of the greatest bass players ever.

Hinton died on December 19, 2000, in New York City.

Herbie Holmes was born in Yazoo City on September 27, 1912. He played in a small combo at Yazoo City High School before graduating in 1929. When he enrolled at the University of Mississippi he joined the college orchestra, The Mississippians, of which he later became a leader.

During Holmes' junior year the NBC radio affiliate in Memphis, WMC, and Loew's State Theater sponsored a vocal competition. Holmes won the first prize, which was a trip to New York, an audition at the NBC studios, and a guest appearance on the Eddie Cantor radio program.

In 1935, his band went on the road, and before long it was the Herbie Holmes Orchestra. In late 1935, the band signed with Music Corporation of America, which handled talent such as Count Basie, Benny Goodman, Tommy Dorsey, and Guy Lombardo.

Gaining more popularity as their tour schedule grew, they changed into a swing-style band playing jazz and Dixieland. Under a new agency, the Frederick Brothers, and with a new vocalist, Nancy Hutson, the orchestra was booked solid playing in fashionable roof gardens of some of the finest hotels.

Holmes adopted the slogan, "Music Served Southern-Style." The press referred to him as "The Young Maestro from the Mississippi Delta." Bassist Fay Anderson from Yazoo City joined the band in 1938. Holmes, Hutson, and the orchestra rang in the New Year 1939 with a national radio broadcast from the Edgewater Beach Hotel in Chicago.

It was about this time when Lawrence Welk, also with the Frederick Brothers Agency, was just starting his act. The agency urged Welk to study Holmes' emcee style and asked Holmes to emulate Welk's musical style. In this way, the Herbie Holmes Orchestra moved away from the Dixieland style and toward a more mellow style of music for dining and dancing.

The band continued to succeed, now

playing in bigger and better hotels. In June 1941, Holmes and Hutson married. Through 1940 and 1941, the band was touring constantly. They recorded four sides for the OKeh label. One side was Holmes' rendition of *Ida,* and Hutson was featured on *A Little Love Is a Dangerous Thing.* Army Brown, later a well-known Jackson businessman, was Holmes' arranger at that time.

During World War II, Holmes became associated with the USO and entertained troops around the country. In 1943, he dissolved the band and joined the Navy. After the war, he, his wife and their two children moved back to Yazoo City, ending his music career. Holmes died on December 1, 1981. In May 1989, he was inducted into the University of Mississippi Jazz Alumni Hall of Fame.

Redd Holt was born in Rosedale on May 16, 1932. He played drums with Ramsey Lewis, El Dee Young, Ken Nordine, and others. He recorded on Argo and Mercury labels.

Holt also worked with David Onderdock, Cleveland Eaton, James Moody, Wallace Burton, John Gray, Chris White, and many others. He can be heard playing drums with April Aloisio, *Brazilian Heart,* released in 1995; Eden Atwood, *No One Ever Tells You,* released in 1992; and Ramsey Lewis, *Down to Earth,* released in 1958.

International Sweethearts of Rhythm was an all-female swing band started at Piney Woods Country Life School, south of Jackson. Piney Woods is a boarding school for students from poor backgrounds at risk of academic failure.

The International Sweethearts of Rhythm was originally organized by Laurence C. Jones, the founder of Piney Woods School, to raise money for the school's operation. The "International" in its name was used because there were women from several foreign countries in the band.

In the late 1930s, the band toured mainly in the South, but slowly began to attract national attention. In 1941, the group made an appearance at the Howard Theater in Washington, D.C. So many people attended that the number of daily shows was increased from five to six. By the end of the week, 35,000 people had come to see the performances, establishing an all-time record. They headlined at the Apollo Theater in 1942.

Also in 1942, the Sweethearts were pitted against Fletcher Henderson's big band in the battle of the sexes before a crowd of 10,000. Similar bookings were made with other male bands, with the Sweethearts often winning the battle.

The band eventually cut ties with Piney Woods School and moved their operation to Arlington, Virginia. The group worked for the USO and entertained servicemen in camps throughout the country as well as overseas. They also performed on Armed Forces Radio Service along with Nat "King" Cole, Lena Horne, Billy Eckstine, and Ella

The International Sweethearts of Rhythm, c. 1942.

Fitzgerald. During that time, they made a six-month tour of France and Germany, playing the Olympia Theater in Paris and the University of Paris.

In 1946, the band recorded for RCA Victor with numbers like *Don't Get It Twisted* and *Vi Vigor*. They also recorded for Guild Records. During that time, the Sweethearts appeared in a series of movie shorts for foreign markets. One was *That Man of Mine*, which starred Ruby Dee.

During the late 1940s, the group continued to tour the U.S. and Canada. In 1984, Rosetta Records re-released a collection of the International Sweethearts of Rhythm numbers.

As a result of the band's performances in the 1940s, it gained the reputation as the best all-female jazz band ever.

Henry "Hank" Jones was born July 31, 1918, in Vicksburg. He played piano in local bands until he moved to New York in 1944. There he played with Hot Lips Page and also worked with greats like Coleman Hawkins, Andy Kirk, and Billy Eckstine. Although his style reflected bebop, he could fit into many genres.

He performed on several Jazz at the Philharmonic tours in 1947 and accompanied Ella Fitzgerald from 1948 to 1953. In the 1950s, Jones performed with Artie Shaw, Benny Goodman, Lester Young, and others. In the late 1970s, he was pianist in the Broadway musical *Ain't Misbehavin'*.

Jones recorded for many labels, including Savoy, Epic, Golden Crest, ABC-Paramount, Muse, and Galaxy. His highest rated album is *The Trio,* released by Savoy in 1955. Others include *Hank Jones Piano* from Mercury in 1950 and *Jazz Trio of Hank Jones* from Monaural in 1955. In fact, Jones appears on some fifty or more albums.

Jimmie Lunceford was born in Fulton, in June, 1902. He studied under Wilberforce Whiteman, father of Paul Whiteman, and earned a degree in music from Fisk University.

He worked in New York with Elmer Snoden and others before taking a teaching position at a high school in Memphis, Tennessee. He formed a band at the school which included Moses Allen, Jimmie Crawford, Willie Smith, and Eddie Wilcox.

When the Jimmie Lunceford Band became popular, Lunceford took the group on tour. In 1929, he went full-time with his band, toured, and broadcasted throughout the Midwest.

In 1933, he reached New York and quickly established a reputation as one of the most popular black bands of the swing era. The arrangers for the band included Eddie Durham and Sy Oliver.

In addition to its powerful sound, the band's showmanship on stage was unique. Members of the trumpet section would toss their horns high into the air and catch them without missing a beat.

The showmanship prompted one writer, George Simon, to say of the Jimmie Lunceford Band, "without a doubt the most exciting big band ever."

Sy Oliver left the band as principal arranger to join Tommy Dorsey. While it was a blow to Lunceford's group, they continued to record and tour. One of their biggest hits was *Tain't What You Do, It's the Way You Do It.*

Lunceford died suddenly in July 1942. His band will be remembered for its unmatched precision and showmanship.

Thomas Hugh "Tom" Malone was born in Hattiesburg, June 16, 1947, but was raised in Sumrall. He played trombone, tuba, piccolo, flute, sax, and electric bass. He arranged and played with Jimmy Dorsey, Woody Herman, Doc Severinsen, and Louis Bellson and played on "The Tonite Show." He recorded on the RCA and Warner Brothers labels.

"Bones" Malone, as he is now called, joined the CBS Orchestra in 1993, playing a variety of instruments, including the trombone, trumpet, and saxophone.

Before joining the CBS group, Malone made more than twenty-five arrangements for "The Late Show" with David Letterman. He may be best known for his work on "Saturday Night Live" as the musical director for the SNL band from

1981-85. He has performed with such acts as James Brown, Pink Floyd, Paul Simon, and Diana Ross.

Malone has played network themes on shows such as "CBS This Morning," "Murder She Wrote," and the 1992 Olympics. He appeared in *The Blues Brothers* movie and has recorded several jazz CDs.

Skeets McWilliams was born August 6, 1924, in Jackson. He started playing the guitar early and went before the public at age eight. That performance was in a shop window in Chicago. He was on the radio in Jackson by age eleven, where he did musical duets with Mundell Lowe.

Skeets McWilliams

His music flowed early from the Armed Forces Radio's "Meet Your Navy" show and from stages with the Ray Anthony Band. Later, he was the fair-haired jazz performer in Chicago's top jazz clubs. He worked at WGN-TV and on the "Lou Payne Show" on WBKB in the 1950s.

A "musician's musician," McWilliams was a mentor to hundreds of guitar students in Jackson. He was friends or mentor to musicians like Bucky Barrett, Lloyd Wells, Mundell Lowe, Steve Blailock, and Bob Saxton.

His career has taken him to some interesting places. He performed the music for a recording of French St. Therese's writings, a Jackson-based group of Carmelite nuns. This project marked the 100th anniversary of the saint's death in 1997.

McWilliams has wide appeal. He has played in England's Sherborne House and teamed up with Bob Saxton to play at the annual three-day Chet Atkins Appreciation Society in 1995.

Country Music magazine said, "Skeets' music is the music of musicians and no matter what your taste in music, Skeets will appeal to you."

He was one of only five Americans selected to participate at the Guitar World Exposition in France.

McWilliams was recently inducted into the Mississippi Musicians Hall of Fame.

Mulgrew Miller was born in Greenwood on August 13, 1955. He began playing piano at an early age. At age twenty-one, he was chosen by Mercer Ellington to fill the chair of Duke Ellington, and he spent three years in that position. He also trained with jazz notables Johnny Griffin, Woody Shaw, Betty Carter, and Tony Williams. He made his debut at the Village Vanguard in New York in 1987. He has worked with Branford Marsalis, Freddie Hubbard, and others.

Miller's albums include *Keys to the City*, released by Landmark in 1985; *Wingspan*, again by Landmark in 1987; and his highest-rated album, *With Our Own Eyes*, released by Jive/Novus in 1993.

Milton Aubrey "Brew" Moore, Jr. was born March 26, 1924, in Indianola. During the period 1942 to 1948, he played tenor sax with local bands in New Orleans and Memphis. He moved to New York in 1948 and played with the Claude Thornhill Orchestra during that time. He played sax in the style of Lester Young. In the early 1950s, he recorded in a session with the great Stan Getz, Al Chon, Zoot Sims, and Allan Eager. He also worked with Machito, Kai Winding, and Gerry Mulligan. He recorded with Stan Getz on *Five Brothers* in 1949.

In 1954, he moved to San Francisco where he led his own group but in 1961 moved to Copenhagen, Denmark, where he stayed until his death. He recorded for Savoy (1948-49), Fantasy (1955-57), Debut, Sonet, and Storyville. Some of his recordings include *Brew Moore Quintet*, released in 1955 on Original Jazz; *Brew Moore in Europe* in 1962 by Fantasy, and his highest-rated album, *I Should Care* (live) by Steeple Chase in 1965.

He died on August 19, 1973, in Copenhagen.

Moon Mullen was born in Mayhew, on May 11, 1916. He played trumpet and composed. He worked with Benny Carter, Louis Armstrong, Cab Calloway, Lionel Hampton, Duke Ellington, and others. He recorded for Hampton and Ellington labels.

Edwin McIntosh "Snoozer" Quinn was born in McComb on October 18, 1906. As a child he played mandolin and violin, and at age seven he took up the guitar. It was not long before he was playing professionally in a local trio in Bogalusa, Louisiana.

In his teens, he worked with the Paul English Traveling Show in a band led by drummer Jack Wilrich. He also played guitar in Claud Blanchard's and Mat Britt's orchestras.

In 1924, he played with cornetist Johnny Wiggs in Peck Kelly's Jazz Band. From late 1925 through 1928, Quinn played around the New Orleans area.

Quinn's most noteworthy engagement was with Paul Whiteman. When Whiteman heard Quinn, he hired him on the spot. He later returned to New Orleans to play with the Red Cap Orchestra.

During his later career, Quinn played guitar, violin, and sang scat vocals in bands led by Earl Crumb. Some compare Quinn's guitar playing to the great Eddie Lang because he played jazz guitar more like a piano with chords rather than single notes.

Some of Quinn's recordings included those done with Paul Whiteman. He played on *Futuristic Rhythm, Raisin' the Roof,* and *Wait Till You See Ma Cherie.* Quinn played backup for Bing Crosby, Tommy Weir, Patsy Young, and Williard Robison.

He also recorded with Jimmie Davis for Victor when Davis sang some of his original compositions like *Hobo's Warning, Bury Me in Old Kentucky, Wild and Reckless Hobo,* and *The Davis Limited.*

In 1948, Quinn recorded *Snoozer's Telephone Blues* on the Wiggs label; later an LP record, *The Legendary Snoozer Quinn,* was released by Fat Cat Jazz Records. Strangely, the last recordings by Quinn were made in the nurses' room in a hospital because he was suffering from tuberculosis.

Quinn died of tuberculosis in New Orleans, Louisiana, in May, 1949.

Emitt Slay was born in Jackson about 1920. This highly skilled, self-taught jazz guitarist traveled and played extensively with the Louis Armstrong Band, then later formed his own trio. He died in Detroit in the 1950s.

Dalton Smith was born and raised in Forest where he learned to play the trumpet in the high school band. After high school, he attended the University of Southern Mississippi where he was first chair in the symphonic and marching bands.

He was lead trumpet player with Stan Kenton in the 1960s and was a freelance studio trumpet player in the 1970s. In the studio, he recorded with Rita Coolidge, Three Dog Night, Glen Campbell, *Cats,* Donna Summer, and Andrae Crouch.

Smith, as a studio trumpet player, can be heard with Glen Campbell, *Rhinestone Cowboy* in 1975; June Christy, *Best of June Christy* in 1949; Nat "King" Cole, *Big Band Cole,* 1950: and Andrae Crouch on *Take Me Back* in 1978.

Sonelius Larel Smith was born in Hillhouse on December 17, 1942. He played piano with John Stubberfield, Frank Foster, H. Vick, D. Byrd, Elvin Jones, and Lionel Hampton. He composed and scored for TV documentaries and for the "Today Show." He also wrote thirteen songs and many more tunes. He recorded for Strata-East and Atlantic labels.

Some of the recordings he performed on include *Navigator* with Andrew Cyrille, *Blacknuss* with Rahsaan Roland Kirk, *Big Band* conducted by Butch Morris, and *Handscapes,* where he played piano and percussion.

Wadada Leo Smith was born in Leland on December 18, 1941. His early musical training began in the high school concert and marching bands. He played trumpet and piccolo and composed. He became interested in the Delta blues and improvisation.

He received his music education from his father, the U.S. Military band program, Sherwood School of Music, and Wesleyan University.

Smith developed a jazz and world music theory which he called, "Ankhrasmation." He has taught at the University of New Haven, Creative Music Studio in Woodstock, New York; and Bard College in New York. He played with the Creative Construction Company, Marion Brown, and Miles Davis. He appeared on TV in France, Germany, and Holland and recorded on Kabell, Delmark, JCOA, and Sackville. His CDs include *Wadada Leo Smith, Kulture of Jazz* on ECM Records.

Frederic Douglas "Freddie" Waits was born on April 27, 1943, in Jackson. He played flute in high school and college and even majored in flute at Jackson State University. He soon became interested in the drums and began playing blues with Memphis Slim and John Lee Hooker. In Detroit in 1962, he was in Paul Winter's band and in Los Angeles and he played in Gerald Wilson's Orchestra before moving to New York in the mid 1960s. Waits associated with Sonny Rollins, Andrew Hill, McCoy Tyner, and Max Roach in the mid- and late 1960s.

He performed with greats like Ella Fitzgerald, Joe Williams, Carmen McRae, The Boston Pops, and the Radio City orchestra.

While Waits did not record on his own, he performed on many recordings by major jazz artists of the day. He can be heard on recordings by Roy Ayers, Kenny Barron, Gary Bartz, Willie Bobo, Ray Bryant, and Kenny Burrell.

Waits died November 18, 1989, in New York.

> **Mississippi First:**
> CASSANDRA WILSON HAS BEEN SELECTED AS *DOWN BEAT'S* JAZZ VOCALIST SO MANY TIMES, SHE IS NOW DESCRIBED AS THE "FIRST LADY OF JAZZ."

Cassandra Wilson was born in Jackson in 1955. She has been singing and performing since age five when she sang at her brother's kindergarten graduation. The youngest of three children, Wilson began playing the piano and guitar at the age of nine.

As far as music is concerned, Wilson credits her interest in music to her mother, a retired elementary schoolteacher, and father, a bass guitarist. Her father introduced her to jazz. In the eleventh grade, she got the leading role as Dorothy in *The Wizard of Oz*. Wilson turned to jazz after graduating from Jackson State University in 1981 and taking a public

Cassandra Wilson, First Lady of Jazz.

affairs director's job for a New Orleans TV station. The following year, 1982, she moved to New York and started working as a vocalist. She began recording widely in the 1980s, initially with Steve Coleman and Henry Threadgill's New Air group. She became the featured vocalist with their M/Base collection.

During her first decade in New York, she released seven records on the JMT/Verve label including *Day Aweigh* and *Point of View* in 1987. By 1993, she had sung on ten albums, like *Dance to Drums Again,* produced by JMT records with a wide variety of New York musicians, including Mulgrew Miller and Greg Osby. Wilson's emotional range and tone variations impress many critics, audiences, and fellow musicians.

She has received many awards. In her hometown of Jackson, she received the 1997 Governor's Award for Excellence in the Arts. Her tour Blood on the Fields was Grammy-nominated for best vocal performance. Wilson won the Best Jazz Vocalist Grammy award for her album *New Moon Daughter.*

Wilson's album *Blue Light 'Til Dawn* was so successful, with more than 600,000 units sold, that it won her *Down Beat's* Singer of the Year title for 1994 and 1995. In 1996, the album also won her the same honor in *Down Beat's* Critic poll. She was named "most important and daring jazz vocalist" by *Time* magazine in 1996. She wrote lyrics for five Miles Davis tunes and wrote four new songs that are Davis-inspired for an album, *Traveling Miles.* Other of her albums include *Blue Skies* in 1987, *Jump World* in 1990, *She Who Weeps* in 1991, and *Best of Genre, Songbook* in 1996. Wilson stays busy singing at all the major jazz festivals and has been selected *Down Beat's* jazz vocalist so many times that she is now described as the "First Lady of Jazz."

Gerald Stanley Wilson was born on September 4, 1918, in Shelby. He learned to play trumpet, began to compose, and eventually became a band leader. He played with the Plantation Music Orchestra early in his career. Upon moving from Memphis to Detroit with his family in 1932, he played with the Jimmie Lunceford Band in 1939 to 1942. Lunceford is also from Mississippi.

He replaced Sy Oliver as arranger, conductor, and trumpet soloist with Lunceford's band. Later, he moved to Los Angeles to play with Les Hite, Benny Carter, and Willie Smith. Wilson organized his own band in 1944, featuring swing and bop. His band attracted many great musicians like Melba Liston and Snooky Young. His bands have performed and recorded throughout the years in the Los Angeles area.

He has played and composed for Count Basie, Earl Carruthers, Stan Kenton, Al Porcino, and the Los Angeles Philharmonic Orchestra. His albums include *Cruisin' with Gerald* in 1945, the highly rated *Moment of Truth* in 1962, *Orchestra of the Eighties* in 1983, and *Theme from Monterey* in 1998. His box compilations include *The Best of the*

Gerald Wilson Orchestra, released in 1961 and 1978, and *Gerald Wilson and His Orchestra: 1945-1946,* released in 1998.

In 1997, Wilson was commisioned by the Monterey Jazz Festival to write an original piece to be perfomed at the festival that year. That piece, *Theme for Monterey*, was recorded and released on an album of the same name in 1998.

Lester Young was born in Woodville on August 27, 1909. Young was taught how to play music by his father, Willis Handy Young. He played the violin, trumpet, and drums, but later focused on the alto saxophone, despite his love for drums.

> •••••
> ## Mississippi First:
> LESTER "THE PREZ" YOUNG, BORN IN WOODVILLE, WAS VOTED GREATEST TENOR SAXOPHONIST EVER; HE WAS THE FIRST TO IMPLEMENT THE "COOL" STYLE OF JAZZ.
> •••••

When he was eleven years old, Young and his father moved to Minneapolis, where they formed a family band. Young, at age thirteen, played alto saxophone. After several disagreements with his father, he left home when he was nineteen.

Young went to play with Art Bronson in Phoenix, Arizona. He played with Bronson until 1930, when he moved back to Minneapolis and played with various bands.

In 1932, while playing at a club with Frank Hines, Young was signed as a member of The Thirteen Original Blue Devils. He and the other band members moved to Kansas City to join Bennie Moten near the end of 1933.

During the years following 1933, Young played in bands like Bennie Moten, George Lee, King Oliver, Count Basie, Fletcher Henderson, Andy Kirk, and many others. In 1936 when Young rejoined Count Basie, he rose to national fame for the first time. Young's rising fame was significant in making Kansas City a major jazz city.

For the next several years, he and Basie toured and recorded. He recorded with Billie Holiday, who gave him the nickname "The Prez." In the early 1940s, Young played in small bands in the Los Angeles area alongside his brother, Lee Young, and musicians such as Red Callender, Nat "King" Cole, and Al Sears. During this period, he returned briefly to the Basie band to record, and he also worked with Dizzy Gillespie.

In the mid-1940s, he was filmed by Gjon Mili in the classic jazz short, *Jammin' The Blues,* a venture which was co-produced by Norman Granz. At this time, he also joined Granz's "Jazz at the Philharmonic," and remained with the organization for a number of years. He also led small groups for club and record dates, toured the U.S., and visited Europe. Young's style was the traditional swing style that will always be linked with Basie's bands. Several famous musicians, including Charlie Parker, Dexter Gordon, and Al Cohn were greatly influenced by Young. He gradually moved toward his famous soft tone that inspired great sax players like Stan Getz.

In the late 1950s, Lester began to have health problems. He was featured on television's "The Sound of Jazz" in 1957 and went on tour with Miles Davis. *The Encyclopedia Yearbook of Jazz* named Lester Young the greatest tenor saxophone player ever in 1956.

Young's discography lists sixty-five albums starting in 1936 with *Young Lester Young* for Columbia Records and ending with a release after his death, *Lester Young and the Kansas City Five* in 1962 on Commodore Records.

Several of his highest-rated albums include *The Jazz Giants '56* on Verve and *Lester Young in Washington* (live) in 1956, released by Pablo.

Young died on March 15, 1959.

He was recently inducted into the Mississippi Musicians Hall of Fame.

Motion Pictures and Television
·····

Mississippians have been writing music for movies and television for years. Although many have achieved great success, they do not have household names like Elvis or B. B. King. These artists perform their craft behind the scenes and yet, their music is heard by millions the world over.

   Most of the musicians described in this section started out on one instrument and eventually branched out into composing and arranging. Their career paths took them to Hollywood and to the small and large screens.

Glen Ballard

Glen Ballard was born in Natchez in 1953. He learned to play the piano early in life and added the guitar later. At ten, he wrote his first song and beginning in the fifth grade, was playing in local rock bands.

Ballard attended the University of Mississippi where he majored in English, political science, and journalism. He graduated with honors and in 1975, moved to Los Angeles where he worked as a songwriter.

After moving to the West coast, Ballard joined Elton John's organization in Los Angeles. Ballard eventually played piano for Kiki Dee. Dee recorded Ballard's song *One Step* in 1978, giving him his first record single.

His success enabled him to secure a professional songwriting job at MCA Music Publishing. During the 1970s and 1980s, Ballard composed many songs, including *What's on Your Mind*, a Quincy Jones-produced hit for George Benson. Thanks to Jones, Ballard's *Try Your Love Again* appeared on James Ingram's 1983 debut album, *It's Your Night*.

Ballard wrote and produced two tracks for Patti Austin entitled *It's Gonna Be Special* and *Shoot the Moon*. By the time Austin's album was released in 1985, Ballard was writing and producing full time for his mentor, Quincy Jones, at Quest Records. He produced for rhythm and blues artists Evelyn "Champagne" King, Teddy Pendergrass, and Jack Wagner. Ballard wrote *All I Need* for Wagner, and it went to the top of *Billboard's* pop chart.

On his own, he had a No. 1 hit with George Strait, *You Looked So Good in Love,* that became the 1986 country song of the year. The same year he co-wrote *Man in the Mirror* which appeared on *Bad,* Michael Jackson's acclaimed follow-up album to *Thriller.*

Man in the Mirror, also produced by Quincy Jones, went to the top of the rhythm and blues charts. Today it remains one of Ballard's most popular songs.

Ballard has worked with some of the biggest names in the industry such as Aretha Franklin, Natalie Cole, Michael Jackson, Quincy Jones, George Strait, and Barbra Streisand. He is also credited with launching debuts by Curtis Stigers, Jack Wagner, Paula Abdul, Wilson Phillips, and the multi-grammy winner, Alanis Morissette. Ballard co-wrote and produced *Jagged Little Pill* for Morissette.

He followed his collaboration with Morissette by producing an Aerosmith album. His talent has resulted in five Grammy nominations and three wins. He has performed on or produced the following: *1997 Grammy Nominees* (1997), *Jagged Little Pill* (1995), *My Cherie* (1995), *Naked And Sacred* (1995), *Time Was* (1995), *Alone in a Crowd* (1993), *Greatest Hits: Songs From An Aging Sex Bomb* (1993), *Lea Salonga* (1993), *Love Come Down: The Best of Evelyn "Champagne" King* (1993), *Shadows And Light* (1992), *Trey Lorenz* (1992), *Curtis Stigers* (1991), *Shut Up And Dance* (1990), *Forever Your Girl* (1989), *Bad* (1987), *Workin' It Back* (1985), *Break Out* (1983), *All I Need,* and *Lighting Up the Night.*

Ballard has written an original screenplay, *Clubland,* and has written songs in six films, including *The Slugger's Wife, Navy Seals,* and *Batman: Mask of the Phantasm.*

Dee Barton was born in Houston, Mississippi, in 1937, but his family moved to Starkville when he was four. He played trombone and drums in the high school band where his father was director.

When he was in high school, his father became ill; and Dee, while still in high school, took over as band director. The band, under his direction, continued the tradition of rating superior at state band contests.

After graduating from Starkville High School in 1955, he attended North Texas State University where he received a bachelor's degree in

Dee Barton

PHOTO COURTESY OF ELWIN WILLIAMS

121 • MOVIES AND TELEVISION

education in 1960 with an emphasis on musical composition. In 1961, he joined the Stan Kenton Orchestra, where he played trombone and drums throughout most of the 1960s (Barton may be the only musician to play and record with two distinct solo instruments in a major big band).

Stan Kenton recorded and released *The Compositions of Dee Barton* in 1968. That album has been described as one of the best Stan Kenton ever did. It set a new direction and style for Kenton and changed the course for big band jazz.

Barton then formed his own Dee Barton Orchestra, a twenty-two piece band which made a big impact in Los Angeles. Clint Eastwood came to hear the band as did many other Hollywood celebrities.

He composed, arranged, conducted, and was a musical consultant for big names such as Tony Bennett, Frank Sinatra, Peggy Lee, John Lennon, and The Rolling Stones.

Clint Eastwood gave Barton his first big break in the movies when he hired him to score the music for the 1971 movie *Play Misty For Me*. He went on to write scores to more than fifty other movies, including three more Clint Eastwood hits, *High Plains Drifter* (1973), *Every Which Way But Loose* (1978), and *Thunderbolt and Lightfoot* (1974).

Barton wrote supplemental compositions for all of Eastwood's five Dirty Harry movies—*Dirty Harry* (1971), *Magnum Force* (1973), *The Enforcer* (1976), *Sudden Impact* (1983), and *The Dead Pool* (1988).

He has written scores for TV shows, including "The Odd Couple," "Red Skelton," "The Rockford Files," "Soul Train," and "Batman." He has also written thousands of TV and radio commercials.

Barton moved back to Mississippi in late 1994 and settled in Jackson. He still does movies in Hollywood and England on a commute-basis.

Barton has been inducted into the Mississippi Musicians Hall of Fame.

Mundell Lowe was born in Laurel on April 22, 1922. Lowe left home at age thirteen. After working in Nashville, he later found his way to New Orleans, where he began his jazz career.

Lowe served in World War II where he played with Ray McKinley's big band. After the war, he moved to New York.

While in New York, he worked for NBC and CBS and appeared on early morning TV shows like "A Date in Manhattan" and "The Kate Smith Hour." It was at that time that he played with Stan Getz, Doc Severinsen, and Kai Winding.

Lowe played guitar and composed for TV and movies. His credits include composing for "I Dream of Jeannie," "Wild, Wild West," "Hawaii 5-0," and movie scores like *Billy Jack*. He toured worldwide with Peggy Lee, Betty Bennett, and the Andre Previn Trio.

Early in his career, he lived and worked in New York City as a studio

Mundell Lowe

musician and composer for CBS and NBC. Considered one of the greatest jazz guitarists in the world, he recorded for over sixteen labels including RCA Records, Warner Brothers Records, Famous Door, Dutch Gramophone, and Verve Records.

In 1965, Lowe moved to Los Angeles and started composing for movies and TV. His television credits include the "Andersonville Trial," "Love on a Rooftop," "The Courtship of Eddie's Father," "Starsky and Hutch," "Andy Griffith Special," "Lucy Comes to Nashville," and "Strike Force."

His movie credits include *In Name Only* for Screen Gems, *Everything You Always Wanted To Know About Sex* with Woody Allen, and *Sidewinders* for 20th Century Fox.

Lowe wants to be most remembered for his work in jazz, which is his first love. He has continued to tour with the Andre Previn Trio in Europe and has worked with Ron Carter, Al Foster, Bill Mays, and Ray Drummond.

Lowe was recently inducted into the Mississippi Musicians Hall of Fame.

Musical Theater, Broadway

Mississippians have had a major impact on musical theater and Broadway since the 1930s. At least for a segment of Mississippi's youth, high school band and music programs provide opportunities for musical growth.

It is also hard for some to imagine that such a Broadway legend as Lehman Engel could have come from Mississippi. But, indeed, Mississippians have played a major role in theater and Broadway and are still making a contribution.

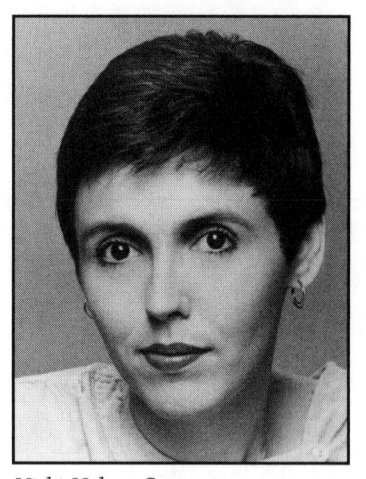

Vicki Helms Carter was born in Tupelo. Her introduction to musical theater came in high school, where she performed in *The Sound of Music* and *The Boyfriend*.

Vicki Helms Carter

She graduated from the University of Southern Mississippi, majoring in piano. While her husband was stationed in North Carolina in the Army, Carter became director of the Ft. Bragg Playhouse. She then moved to New York in hopes of a career in music.

In New York, she was pianist for the production of *Jacques Brel Is Alive and Well and Living in Paris*. She conducted off-Broadway productions including *Shuffle Along* and then the big Broadway smash *Eubie!* in 1978. In just two years, Carter had made it to Broadway.

Her involvement in *Eubie!* brought a letter from President Carter thanking her for honoring the Vice-Premier of the People's Republic of China with the performance.

Carter was the musical director and conductor of the premiere performance of *Huck and Jim on the Mississippi* in 1983, which was written by Joshua Logan.

She has more recently become involved in industrial conventions. Her productions have been heard by GMC Truck dealers and by Rotary International. In addition, her work has been presented for the National Association of Food Brokers, National Association of Tobacco Dealers, and Merle Norman Cosmetics.

She and her husband helped originate the Mississippi Picnic which is held each year in New York City.

Lehman Engel was born in 1910 in Jackson. While in high school, he wrote the *Central High School Alma Mater.* He attended the Cincinnati Conservatory of Music and the Juilliard Graduate School in 1935. He also studied composition with Roger Sessions.

Engel was a dynamo of musical activity. He conducted more than thirty-five musicals including *Oklahoma, Guys and Dolls,* and *West Side Story.* He composed more than thirty-four incidental music numbers including *Julius Caesar, The Wisteria Trees,* and *Anne of the Thousand Days.*

Engel composed and conducted more than thirty-four musicals including *Macbeth, Hamlet,* and *Within the Gates.* He conducted on more than sixty-six recordings, twenty-three radio and TV programs, and fourteen films. His radio experience included the Texaco series on CBS with Charles Laughton, Frederic March, Helen Hayes, Ethel Barrymore, and many more.

His television work included the "Hallmark Hall of Fame," "Texaco's

Lehman Engel

Command Appearance," and "The Tempest" for NBC. His films included *Strategic Attack* for RKO, *Strange Victory* for Target, and *Beyond Gauguin* for which he composed and conducted the score.

His awards included the 1964 Henry Bellamann Foundation Award, Antoinette Perry (Tony) Award for *Wonderful Town,* and the Society for the Publication of American Music Award in 1946.

He also received a decoration from the Republic of Austria, Honorary Doctorate of Music from the University of Cincinnati, ASCAP's Deems Taylor Award, and the Consular Law Society Award for Outstanding Achievement in the Theater.

He wrote thirteen books and produced numerous lectures, workshops and articles. Lehman Engel workshops are still being held throughout the country.

Engel was truly a giant in musical theater and served in that capacity for more than fifty years. Engel died in 1982 and is buried in his hometown of Jackson.

Engel was recently inducted into the Mississippi Musicians Hall of Fame.

127 • MUSICAL THEATER

Mary Ann Mobley

Mary Ann Mobley was born in Brandon on February 17, 1939. She was in the Lions All-State Band in high school and became Miss America in 1959. She received one of the highest scores in that contest ever up until that time.

After finishing her year as Miss America, she made her Broadway debut in the play *Nowhere to Go But Up*. She also appeared in off-Broadway productions of *The King And I*, *Oklahoma*, *Cabaret*, and *Hello, Dolly*.

She went to Hollywood in the early 1960s where she danced and sang with Elvis Presley in back-to-back movie musicals, *Girl Happy* and *Harum Scarum*.

Mobley has made numerous TV appearances including "Girl From Uncle." She maintains close ties with Mississippi, where she and her husband, actor Gary Collins, help with many charity events.

Lloyd Wells was born April 22, 1938, and is a native of Laurel. He graduated from the University of Southern Mississippi with a degree in Music Education in 1960. He became band director at the South Pike Consolidated High School in Magnolia and stayed there until 1964.

Upon the advice of Mundell Lowe, he moved to New York in 1964 and found work as a guitarist on Broadway and TV. Wells was a guitarist in Broadway shows such as *The Yearling, Skyscraper, Superman, Cabaret, Golden Rainbow, Zorba, Company, La Strada, The Selling of the President,* and *Two Gentlemen of Verona.*

Wells worked with many top artists including Peggy Lee, Glenn Miller Band, Les and Larry Elgart Band, Sammy Kaye Band, Rosemary Clooney, Guy Mitchell, Jane Russell, and Tennessee Ernie Ford. He toured extensively with Ford during the 1970s and 1980s.

He has also used his guitar skills on "Sesame Street," "Electric Company,"

Lloyd Wells

"Merv Griffin Show," "Ed Sullivan Show," "Johnny Carson," and "Skitch Henderson Show."

He moved to Nashville in 1976 where he joined Opryland USA as music director. He produced, arranged, and composed more than 200 musical shows for Opryland. In addition, he was band leader for Opryland's Country Music USA tour to Russia. He was music director and conductor for Celebration of the Centuries, Tennessee's celebration of 200 years of statehood.

He has also directed park shows in Branson, Missouri; Gatlinburg, Tennessee; Hot Springs, Arkansas; and Louisville, Kentucky. He has written, conducted, and arranged many shows for industry, television, and entertainment parks. He has made appearances on "Hee Haw," "Nashville Now," and the "CMA Awards."

Wells arranged and conducted the only official Gershwin estate-sanctioned Gershwin Review that played in ninety cities.

Wells was recently inducted into the Mississippi Musicians Hall of Fame.

Popular (Pop)

Popular or "pop" music is a hard category to define. It is essentially whatever is most popular with the public at any given time. Pop music embraces many different genres of music and has been around for at least fifty years.

During the period 1900 to 1950, pop included blues, jazz, standards, big band, and country. From the 1950s to the present, pop has included rock and roll, rhythm and blues, love songs, folk, disco, and hip hop.

Today, pop music has many styles, including contemporary, pop/rock, country, Brit, Latin and many other forms.

For the sake of this chapter, pop music performers are included where there are no other chapters covering their genres. Nevertheless, they are still classified as pop or popular artists even though their styles are vastly different.

William Alexander Attaway was born in Greenville on November 19, 1911, to William S. Attaway, a medical doctor, and Florence Parry Attaway, a teacher. At the age of six, his family moved to Chicago, Illinois where he later attended a vocational high school. Upon graduation, Attaway enrolled at the University of Illinois.

The death of Attaway's father forced him to drop out of college. Attaway returned to the University of Illinois in 1935, received his degree, and moved to New York. In 1936, Attaway published his first story "Tale of the Blackamoor."

In 1939, he learned that his first novel, Let Me Breathe Thunder, had been accepted for publication. Aided by a two-year grant from the Julius Rosenwald Fund, Attaway immediately began work on his next novel, Blood on the Forge, which was published in 1941.

After Blood on the Forge was published, Attaway wrote songs, books about music, and screenplays. In 1957, Calypso Song Book, a collection of songs, was produced. In 1967, he wrote Hear America Singing, a children's history of popular music in America. Attaway wrote songs for Harry Belafonte, including the famous Day-O Banana Boat Song. Altogether, Attaway wrote more than 500 songs.

In the 1950s, he turned to writing for radio, films, and TV. He wrote for such TV programs as "Wide Wide World" and the "Colgate Hour." Attaway was the first black writer to write scripts for TV and films. He wrote "Hundred Years of Laughter," an hour-long special on black humor that aired in 1964. The special featured comedians Redd Foxx, Moms Mabley, and Flip Wilson in their first appearance on television.

His last years were spent in California writing screenplays. He died of cancer in June 1986.

James Lansten "Lance" Bass was born May 4, 1979, to Jim and Diane Bass of Laurel. He has one older sister, Stacy. In 1989, Jim Bass moved his family to Clinton. Bass began singing in the chorus when he was in the seventh grade.

In eighth grade, Bass auditioned for and made the Mississippi Show Stoppers, a statewide group sponsored by the Mississippi Agricultural and Forestry Museum. At Clinton High School, Bass later became a member of a competition choir called Attache, a nationally recognized high school competition show group.

Bass now sings with 'N Sync, a pop and dance group signed to BMG in Germany. In that country, they racked up gold records and had a No. 1 album. 'N Sync is composed of four other young men, all from different backgrounds. Bass was chosen for the group even though he did not audition. Bass is the "bass" singer of 'N Sync.

The group has been compared to such groups as the Backstreet Boys and New Kids On The Block. 'N Sync was first a hit in Europe but eventually became popular in America, partially due to their Disney Channel live concert. 'N Sync's

Lance Bass (center) and 'N Sync.

self-titled debut album was released on March 24, 1998.

'N Sync features dance, singing, lasers, pyrotechnics, and many wardrobe changes in their live performances. They play to sold-out shows wherever they go. Ticket sales sometimes reach 600,000 in advance of a tour.

Their first single was *I Want You Back*. It was the fastest-rising single and had the longest stay for a new act on the charts. *I Want You Back* went platinum within four months of its release. It went double platinum in Canada.

In November 1998, 'N Sync had two albums on the *Billboard* Top 10 Chart. Their *Tearin' Up My Heart* and *I Want You Back* are hits on pop, rhythm, and mainstream charts. Their album, *No Strings Attached,* sold 2.4 million copies in its first week of release.

The group has its own line of products which includes pillows, pencils, T-shirts and trading cards. Their work schedule included a forty-one-city tour in 2000 and appearances on the "Miss Universe Contest" television show.

Bass and 'N Sync are so popular that their memorabilia are currently sold at very high prices. For example, a water bottle used by one of the group during a concert sold for $500.

'N Sync was voted Internet Artist of the Year at the 2001 American Music Awards, the first category if its kind.

Bass has started his own record label, Free Lance Entertainment, to help young artists. The first to be signed was sixteen-year-old Meredith Edwards of Clinton.

Guy Lee Hovis, Jr., was born September 24, 1941, in Tupelo. He attended the University of Mississippi where he studied accounting. While at Ole Miss he and three Ole Miss fraternity brothers—Allen Pepper, Trent Lott, and Gaylen Roberts—formed a music group and called themselves the Chancellers. Hovis went to Los Angeles after he graduated and two years later joined the Army where he did a tour in Vietnam.

Guy Hovis

Prior to serving in the Army, Hovis had appeared on Art Linkletter's show "House Party" and was part of a duo known as Guy and Davis for ABC Records. He appeared with stars like Johnny Carson, Mike Douglas, Merv Griffin, Jim Nabors, Bob Hope, and Dinah Shore. Hovis was nominated by members in the recording industry as both producer and artist of the year. In 1970, he joined the "Lawrence Welk Show" and stayed through 1982. He recorded fifteen albums, among them *Give Me That Old Time Religion* in 1964 and *Best Loved Hymns* in 1995. The Welk show was canceled in 1982, but the cast continued to give live performances until 1988. In 1989, Guy returned to Mississippi when his old friend U.S. Senator Trent Lott asked him to act as his Mississippi office director. Hovis lives in Jackson and still does some recording. Hovis still performs two times a year at the Lawrence Welk Theater in Branson, Missouri. He does concerts for festivals and churches.

Van Dyke Parks was born January 3, 1941, in Hattiesburg. He moved with his family to Hollywood at age thirteen and became a child actor while studying classical piano and composition. In the early 1960s, he signed with MGM Studios to write soundtrack music for Walt Disney films. Instead, he began writing his own songs, one of which, *High Coin,* has become a folk rock standard and was covered by Bobby Vee, Harper's Bizarre, and the Charlatans, among others. In the mid-1960s, he produced such hits as the Mojo Men's cover of Stephen Stills' *Sit Down I Think I Love You* and Harper's Bizarre's cover of Cole Porter's *Anything Goes.*

In 1966, Parks began collaborating with Brian Wilson of the Beach Boys on the never released *Smile* (e.g. *Heroes And Villains*). Some of the songs appeared on later Beach Boys albums/singles. His own first solo LP, *Song Cycle,* was an ambitious and eclectic project complete with lavish arrangements and unusual vocal treatments. Four years in the making, it was hailed as the first "art rock" LP and considered a masterpiece by many. He produced or arranged for Randy

Van Dyke Parks

Newman (1968), as well as Judy Collins, Ry Cooder, Phil Ochs, Arlo Guthrie, Manhattan Transfer, Gordon Lightfoot, Ringo Starr, Carly Simon, and others. He did sessions on piano with Tim Buckley, Little Feat, and The Byrds on *Eight Miles High.*

Parks was director of audiovisual services for Warner Brothers in 1970, a post he quit a year later. He then immersed himself in Caribbean music, produced calypso king Mighty Sparrow, *Hot and Sweet* (1974) and the Esso Trinidad Steel Band, which also appeared on his *Discover America* album. His third album, *The Clang of The Yankee Reaper,* was more straightforward; then there was his fourth, entitled *Jump!.* It returned him in spirit and feel to his Mississippi roots, having been based on the nursery rhymes and children's stories of Joel Chandler Harris' *Tales of Uncle Remus.* His first three LPs were reissued on Edsel in the UK in 1986 to unexpected critical acclaim. He played keyboards on the soundtrack for Robert Altman's *Popeye,* in which he also briefly appeared.

Another album in 1989 was *Tokyo Rose* that concerned the state of American-Japanese relations. He toured with Ry Cooder in 1988 and has scored countless television shows and films since. He wrote and scored for a Summer 2000 tour for Brian Wilson.

His fifth album, *Moonlighting: Live At The Ash Grove,* features older tunes and playful songs like CHICKEN.

He made appearances on recordings with The Beach Boys, The Byrds, Judy Collins, Ry Cooder, Kathy Dalton, Dirty Looks, and the Divinyls. He has songs on albums by The Beach Boys, Charlatans, Harpers Bizarre, Jan & Dean, and Candye Kane.

He has written TV and film music for "Sesame Street," "Melrose Place," *The Two Jakes, Popeye,* and *Private Parts.*

Parks operates on the fringe of popular music with a low profile but unusually high credits. His specialty in the music business as songwriter, lyricist, arranger, and producer is dense aural and verbal montages, which are most easily sampled in his lyrics for the Beach Boys' *Heroes and Villains* or *Surf's Up.*

Nanette Workman was born in New York and raised in Jackson. She was the daughter of a musical family with her mother a singer and her father an instrumental band conductor.

After attending the University of Southern Mississippi for a short time in 1963, Workman was persuaded to go to New York by Arthur Rubinstein, Jr., who heard her sing at a synagogue in Jackson.

She landed a role as understudy to the leading lady in the Broadway musical,

Nanette Workman

How to Succeed in Business Without Really Trying, and played the lead for two weeks and in summer stock.

Her first single was produced by Tony Roman and was No. 1 on the charts for fifteen weeks in Canada. She remained in Quebec for two years where she recorded, appeared on all the popular TV shows, and hosted her own television show for CBC.

Workman went to England where she had a weekly spot on Peter Cook and Dudley Moore's comedy series. She is the voice behind Mick Jagger on The Rolling Stones' album *Let it Bleed* and several other albums. In England, she worked with John Lennon, Ringo Starr, George Harrison, and many other popular British recording stars.

She then went to France and worked with superstar Johnny Hallyday. She joined Hallyday on a world tour as his opening act. Workman recorded another album in England, then returned to Quebec and recorded several more albums in French.

Back in France, she starred in the Rock Opera *Starmania* and in another opera in Paris, *La Legend de Jimmy.* She has also appeared in many commercials and popular TV shows in Canada, England, and France.

Workman has appeared in many films, including *Mustang, Scandals, Evil Judgement, Caravans, NBC Movie of the Week, C.A.T. Squad,* and more recently, *The Ladies Room,* which co-starred John Malkovich and Lorraine Bracco.

Workman's success in England, France, and Canada has been compared to the popularity of the singer Cher in the U.S. Perhaps now she will gain the recognition she deserves in this country.

Workman was recently inducted into the Mississippi Musicians Hall of Fame.

Production, Recording and Promotion

•••••

It may be argued that this category is not for musicians, per se. However, without the help and encouragement of record companies, promoters, talent scouts, and instrument makers, Mississippi musicians may never have been heard.

It can also be argued that in the 1920s and 1930s, Mississippi talent scouts like Jackson's H. C. Speir contributed as much to the discovery of musical talent as those in Nashville and Memphis.

To this day, major record labels and instrument manufacturers flourish in Mississippi.

Delta Records, owned and operated by Jimmie Ammons of Jackson, was the first recording studio in Mississippi. It was noted for its custom work which included weddings, church and college choirs, LPs for the University of Mississippi Foreign Languages Department, commercials for radio, recording by radio station broadcasts over Mississippi for ASCAP, and on-site recordings of all state university bands. Delta recorded Houston Davis' *Go Mississippi* in 1962 and had its own ASCAP Publishing Company named Ammons Publishing Co.

The first recordings by Ace Records (Johnny Vincent Imbragoulio) and Trumpet (Lillian McMurray) were recorded at Delta. Delta had several labels including Delta, Ala-Miss, Sunset, Magnolia, New World, and Cotton.

Delta also rehearsed bands in the studio, made schedules for dance sets, and booked bands for engagements.

Some of the records cut in the 1950s at Delta Records include Little Milton's *Boogie* and *Boogie Woogie Baby,* Sonny Boy Williamson's *Catfish Blues,* Tommy Lee's *Highway 80 Blues,* The Canton Spirituals' *Wonderful Change,* several recordings by The Williams Brothers, and others.

In October 1957, Delta Records arranged a recording session with Andy Anderson and The Rolling Stones at Owen Bradley's Studio in Nashville. The session included The Jordonaires as back-up to record *Johnny Valentine* and *I I I Love You.*

After The Rolling Stones' record was released, their bookings went from $35 per engagement to $400 and $500 per engagement. The Rolling Stones played at the University of Alabama, Ole Miss, Mississippi State, Louisiana State, Memphis State, and the Neshoba County Fair. After forty years they still play at reunions for their fans. (See Rolling Stones in rock and roll chapter).

Other recording groups for Delta included Emmit Hawkins and His Melody Boys, Milton Beasley and the Country Cowboys, Carlton Wells, Jimmy Baker, Southerners Gospel Quartet, and Rick Richardson.

One band, Warner Mack, could not seem to get the sound they wanted for a recording. Ammons brought in a cattle watering tub and put the microphone inside to get the echo sound the band wanted.

In the late 1950s, there were The Thomas Trio, The Red Counts, Rick and the Rockets, and Cool Cat Cannon and the Crackerjacks. Delta continued to record in the 1960s with Tina and the Tides and in the 1970s with Beaker Street.

John V. Imbragoulio (Johnny Vincent) was born October 3, 1927, and raised in Laurel. He was a man behind the scenes with some of the greatest hits in rock and roll and rhythm and blues.

Imbragoulio was the owner of Ace Records, Ace Music Publishers, and Avanti Records in Pearl. He produced such well-known hits as Huey Smith's *Rockin' Pneumonia and the Boogie Woogie Flu* and

Sea Cruise. *Sea Cruise* remains one of the all-time great rock and roll hits.

His first record label was listed in Art Rupe Speciality Records, and from there, he made Ace Records famous. Ace Records was the only independent record company at the time in New Orleans.

Imbragoulio sold Ace Records and started Avanti Records which featured more rhythm and blues and soul recordings. More recently, he was executive producer for Guitar Slim, John Lee Hooker, Frankie Ford, Willie Clayton, Billy Bonds, and Jimmy Angel.

Imbragoulio died in 1999.

Malaco Records of Jackson was organized by Tommy Couch and Mitchell Malouf in 1968. It takes its name from Mal and Co, the beginning letters of the names of its founders. While at Ole Miss, Couch, Malouf, and Wolf Stephenson began to book rhythm and blues bands for parties and concerts.

As this line of activity became more successful, the boys considered expanding Malaco into the recording business. They had booked such stars as Ray Stevens, Charlie Rich, The Dave Clark 5, Herman's Hermits, and The Who, so why not try recording?

Eventually, Couch, Malouf, and Stephenson ended up in Jackson. The rest of the story is of a thirty-year struggle of a record company that has outlasted many major record labels. Malaco's story is told in *The Last Soul Company* by Rob Bowman, self-published by Malaco in 1999.

Tommy Couch, Malaco Records

Malaco's first gold record was a rhythm and blues number called *Groove Me*. The company has recorded stars like Dorothy Moore, Bobby "Blue" Bland, Johnny Taylor, Z. Z. Hill, Denise LaSalle, and Little Milton Campbell.

In addition to soul, however, it has been very successful recording and promoting gospel artists and groups such as the world-renowned Mississippi Mass Choir.

Other artists and groups recorded by Malaco can be found throughout this book, and Malaco continues to expand its distribution of labels into the worldwide market. CDs and videos are produced by Malaco in a growing number of genres.

Malaco was recently inducted into the Mississippi Musicians Hall of Fame.

Willard and Lillian McMurray of Jackson were the founders of Diamond Records and the Trumpet label. They recorded many well-known national artists such as the Southern Sons Quartet, the St. Andrews Gospelaires, Sonny Boy Williamson, Gees, Tiny Kennedy, and Big Joe Williams.

Peavey Electronics was founded by Hartley Peavey, who was born in Meridian in 1941. He received his business degree from Mississippi State University in 1965.

With only $8,000, he started a company to manufacture electric guitar amplifiers. That company, Peavey Electronics, now exports to 103 countries and has thirty-one plants employing more than 2,300, including one plant in Corby, England.

Peavey Electronics produces more than 3,000 items that range from audio cables to guitars. These products have been seen on TV in "Baywatch," on the floor of the U.S. Senate, and at many rock and roll concerts.

The company has received the U.S. Department of Commerce's Presidential E-Star Award. Peavey Electronics was featured in the Simon and Schuster book, *Making It In America,* along with Xerox, Microsoft, Harley Davidson, and other top firms.

In 1996, Peavey was featured on the Cable News Network program "Pinnacle," seen in 210 countries worldwide. It was rebroadcast on August 24, 1996.

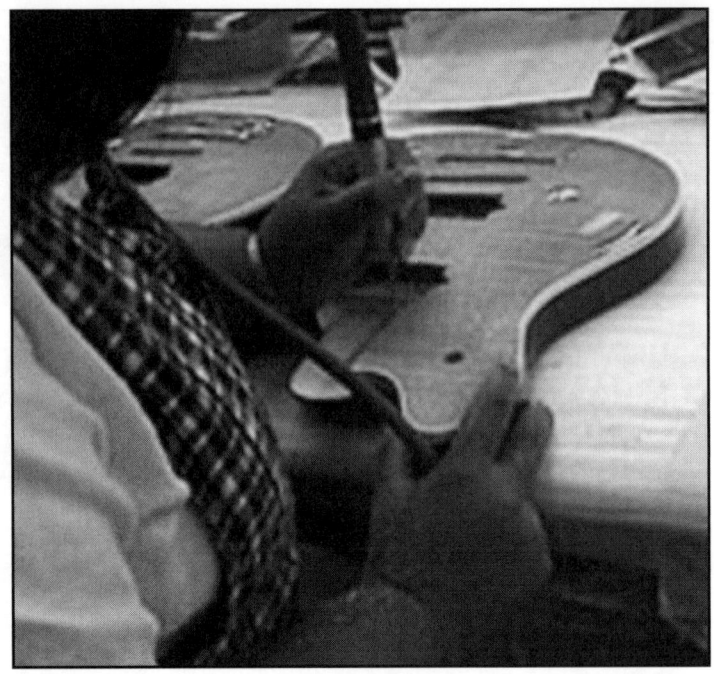

Making a guitar at Peavey Electronics.

Rooster Blues Records of Clarksdale was founded by Jim O'Neal and represented the blues purists. O'Neal was one of the founders of *Living Blues Magazine* in 1970.

Rooster featured stars like Eddie Campbell, Eddy Clearwater, Johnny Littlejohn, Roosevelt "Booba" Barnes, Eddie Shaw, Robert Walker, Lonnie

Shields, Valerie Wellington, Carey Bell, Magic Slim, Casey Jones, and Luther "Guitar Junior" Johnson.

Rooster Records moved its operations from Clarksdale to Kansas City in 1999.

H. C. Speir was a businessman in Jackson. From 1925 to 1935, he was the primary reason so many Mississippi blues artists were "discovered." He became a talent scout for major record companies such as Victor, Columbia, Brunswick, Paramount, and OKeh.

Speir owned a music store in 1925 on Farish Street in Jackson. Because he was interested in helping his business, he started asking musicians to come record their songs. He had one of the few recording machines in the South at that time. He would take the musicians up to the second floor of his music store and make a "demo" for record companies.

Paramount was most involved in Speir's efforts to find talent between 1929 and 1932. They learned to accept his word when he recommended a musician. In fact, Speir found almost all of Paramount's southern talent.

For OKeh in 1930, Speir mastered nearly one hundred records in the King Edward Hotel with such artists as the Mississippi Sheiks, Bo Carter, Charlie McCoy, Slim Duckett and Pig Norwood, Elder Curry, the Campbell College Quartet, Elder Charles Beck, and Mississippi Coleman Bracy and Bracy's wife.

He "found" Delta and regional bluesmen like Charlie Patton, Skip James, Tommy Johnson, Ishmon Bracey, Bo Carter, the Mississippi Sheiks, William Harris, Blind Joe Reynolds, Blind Roosevelt Graves, Washboard Walter, Cheeshie Wiley, Elvie Thomas, Isaiah Nettles, and Robert Wilkins. His influence was indirectly responsible for the success of Son House, Willie Brown, and Robert Johnson. His involvement in these discoveries resulted in more than 200 sides being recorded by now famous bluesmen.

In 1934, he set up a recording session in Jackson in an old dance hall on Farish Street and recorded nearly 120 masters. For that session, he brought in performers from the southern region.

> • • • • •
> **Mississippi First:**
> H. C. SPEIR, OF JACKSON, WAS THE FIRST AND ONLY PERSON TO BE CALLED "GODFATHER OF DELTA BLUES."
> • • • • •

It could be said that Jackson, during the 1930s, was the "Nashville of the South." Under Speir's direction, Jackson was a major producer of musical recording talent.

However, with all of his success at identifying talent, Speir missed on Jimmie Rodgers, whom he told to go home and practice.

With all of these discoveries to his credit, Speir made little money for deals he made with record companies. He

H. C. Speir, *Godfather of the Delta Blues.*

preferred to work on a contract basis, which cut him out of royalty money. He also financed many trips for bluesmen to recording sessions throughout the country.

He gave up the scouting business in 1937 when he thought the recording industry was dead due to a musicians' strike.

The story of H. C. Speir is described in *Chasin' That Devil Music—Searching for The Blues,* edited by Gayle Dean Wardlow and published by Miller Freeman Books.

Speir was deemed the "Godfather of Delta Blues," and was recently inducted into the Mississippi Musicians Hall of Fame.

Speir died in 1972.

Rhythm and Blues, Soul

•••••

There is a close relationship between blues, soul, and rhythm and blues. Rhythm and blues grew out of the blues during the 1940s and 1950s. R&B, as it is called, relies on a band and sometimes backup singers. The music is more emotional and often involves dance and other theatrics.

Soul, on the other hand, followed R&B and has a strong gospel influence. Considered the most emotional and personal of the three, soul relies heavily on horns and backup singers.

Mississippians have had a huge influence on the development of each. In fact, many of the same artists will appear in a list of all three genres: blues, R&B, and soul.

Sam Cooke was born Samuel Cook on January 22, 1931, in Clarksdale. He was one of eight children born to Rev. Charles and Annie Mae Cook. The family moved to Chicago in 1933, and Sam started singing when he was nineteen with a family gospel group called the Soul Stirrers. This group included two of his sisters and one brother.

Cooke performed a pop single called *Loveable* in 1956 on the same Specialty Record label that recorded the Soul Stirrers' music. He used the name "Dale Cooke" on the label to avoid conflict with the family gospel group. Cooke is the composer of numerous songs, including *Another Saturday Night, Bring It on Home to Me, A Change is Gonna Come,* and *Cupid.* His first hit was the 1957 release that he wrote with his brother, L. C. Cooke, *You Send Me.* It sold a million copies in 1957 alone.

RCA Victor signed him in 1960 after he had several rhythm and blues hits for Specialty Records.

Transcending all barriers of race and faith, Cooke is remembered for writing and singing such hit songs as *Only Sixteen, Wonderful World,* and *Chain Gang.*

In the early 1960s, Cooke was also working as a record producer on his own independent label, SAR, which released *Soothe Me* by the Simms Twins and *Rome Wasn't Built in a Day* by Johnny Taylor.

In 1961, he released *Cupid,* his hit song to the Roman god of love. In 1962 he capitalized on the new dance craze, the Twist, with *Twistin' the Night Away. A Change is Gonna Come* and *Shake* were added to his list of hit records after his death on December 11, 1964, in Los Angeles, California.

His albums, many re-releases, include *Two Sides of Sam Cooke* in 1970 by Specialty, *Live at the Harlem Square Club* in 1985 by RCA, *Rhythm and the Blues* in 1995 by RCA, and *Sam Cooke* in 2000 by Wea.

On January 23, 1986, he was inducted into the Rock and Roll Hall of Fame; and on June 15, 1993, he was awarded the Apollo Theater Foundation Chairman Award. Cooke was recently inducted into the Mississippi Musicians Hall of Fame.

Tyrone Davis was born May 4, 1938, in Greenwood. Said to be a smooth soul or pop-soul singer, Davis made his major contribution to music between the 1960s and 1980s with continued success into the 1990s.

Davis appeared on record in 1965 with *Tyrone the Wonder Boy* on the Four Brothers label. For *Can I Change My Mind* in 1968, he changed to the Dakar label for a successful chart-topper. Then came the million-seller classic *Turn Back the Hands of Time* in 1970. Davis remained with Dakar until 1976 with

Sam Cooke

Tyrone Davis

releases of *I Had It All The Time* and *Turning Point*. He then signed with Columbia for new releases but changed labels frequently.

However, he found new success at Malaco with *Simply Tyrone Davis* (1996), *Pleasing You* (1997), and *Call Tyrone* (1999). *Relaxin' With Tyrone* came shortly after that. Davis has worked with Sonny Sanders, Stevie Robinson, Bobby Lewis, Judy Stone, and many more. His many albums include *In the Mood With Tyrone Davis* on Columbia in 1997, *Our Shining Hour* in 1983 on PolyGram, *Come On Over* in 1990 on Future, and *It's So Good* in 1995 on Life.

Bo Diddley was born on December 30, 1928, in McComb. Bo's legal name was Ellas McDaniel, but he was born Otha Ellas Bates. When still a child, McDaniel studied violin and taught himself guitar.

As a young adult, McDaniel earned money working in construction and as a semi-pro boxer. He would also spend time playing music on city streets for extra money. In his early career (1945-1951), he was the lead singer in a washboard trio. McDaniel signed with Chess/Checker Records in 1955 and remained with them until 1974. In 1955, he recorded his first hit song, *I'm a Man,* which was No. 2 on the charts.

He used the stage name Bo Diddley which was taken from a one-stringed African guitar called the "diddley-bow." Diddley has performed for presidents including John Kennedy and George Bush. He also performed at the Democratic National Convention for Bill Clinton.

·····
Mississippi First:
BO DIDDLEY, BORN IN MCCOMB, IS FIRST TO BE CALLED THE "FATHER OF RHYTHM AND BLUES."
·····

Some of his other accomplishments include induction into the Rock and Roll Hall of Fame in 1987, a star on the Hollywood Walk of Fame in 1989, and the Lifetime Achievement Award by the Rhythm and Blues Foundation at the Seventh Annual Pioneer Awards in 1996. Diddley's *Road Runner Live* was released by Mastertone on February 26, 1999. Some of his other hit songs include *Uncle*

Bo Diddley, Father of Rhythm and Blues, playing his signature square guitar.

John; Shave and a Haircut; Cracking Up, Ooh, Baby, Diddley Wah Diddey, and *Hey Bo Diddley.*

He has had a long-lasting career that spans over five decades and his popularity is worldwide. He was recently inducted into the Mississippi Musicians Hall of Fame.

John Lee "Hook" Hooker was born on August 17, 1920, in Clarksdale to a Baptist minister and his wife. At age fourteen, he started singing with spiritual groups. Hooker learned his style of hypnotic one-note guitar playing from his stepfather, Will Moore. He also learned to play from his friends, James Smith and Coot Harris.

Hooker introduced the style that many white blues bands used in playing rhythm and blues and rock and roll. He was the first great recorded user of the electric blues-rock-funk and boogie. He is sometimes called the King of Boogie. When Hooker cut his first single, a boogie called *Boogie Chillen* in 1948, he was working as a janitor in a Detroit steel mill. *Boogie Chillen* made it to the top of the R&B charts. After the song became a hit, Hooker quit his job to play full-time. In 1962, Hooker recorded another smash hit entitled *Boom Boom*. In the late 1970s, Hooker appeared in the hit movie, *The Blues Brothers,* where he sang his hit, *Boom Boom.*

British bands such as The Animals and The Yardbirds idolized Hooker.

In 1960, he performed at the Newport Folk Festival, and in 1973 he was in a concert at Lincoln Center. He has worked with Eric Clapton, Muddy Waters, Albert King, Peg Leg Sam, Ginger Baker, and Chris Wood. He has also worked with a few other rock groups such as The Rolling Stones.

Some of his albums include *Everybody's Blues* in 1950, *That's My Story* in 1960, and *The Real Folk Blues* in 1966.

In 1996, he won a Grammy for Traditional Blues Album and the Blues Foundation's Second Annual Lifetime Achievement Award. He was inducted into the Rock and Roll Hall of Fame and has received the W. C. Handy Blues Award. He will be most remembered for his influence on rhythm and blues and rock and roll.

As of this writing, Hooker is semi-retired and living in California.

Eddie "Guitar Slim" Jones was born on December 10, 1926, and grew up in Hollandale. He played at the Apollo Theater at a young age and is considered a primary figure in rhythm and blues. His R&B classic hit record, *The Things That Used To Be,* topped the R&B charts for six weeks in 1953 and has become a blues standard. (Ray Charles backed him on piano). With his red, blue or green suits and hair to match, he was an unequaled showman. He had hits with *The Things I Do to You, The Story of My Life,* and *Well I Done Got Over It.* He recorded five albums.

Jones died in New York City on February 7, 1959.

Albert King

Albert King was born Albert Nelson in Indianola on April 25, 1923, but moved to Forrest City, Arkansas, where he grew up on a farm. Nelson was a self-taught guitar player who learned how to play on a one string "diddley-bow." At the age of six, he had only a cigar box guitar; twelve years later he got his first real guitar, which cost him one dollar and twenty-five cents. He played guitar left-handed and upside-down without re-stringing the guitar.

Nelson adopted the stage name Albert King after he heard B. B. King's *Three O'Clock Blues*.

He performed with the Yancey's Band, but he kept his day job as a bulldozer driver. In addition to his performing with the Yancey's Band, he sat in with the Grove Boys. In 1953, he moved to Gary, Indiana; here he sang with the Harmony Boys, which featured bluesmen Jimmy Reed, Brook Benton, John Brim, and Jackie Wilson.

King was a major influence on blues and rock guitar players like Stevie Ray Vaughan, Robert Cray, Otis Rush, Eric Clapton, and others. In fact, Clapton copied King's *Personal Manager* guitar solo note-for-note on Cream's song *Strange Brew*.

Some of his singles were *Bad Luck Blues* and *Be on Your Merry Way*. The song *Don't Throw Your Love on Me So Strong* became No. 14 on the Top 20 blues hit list. King's biggest success came when he signed with Stax Records in 1966, where he recorded with the house band Booker T. and the MGs.

King made a good career move when he signed with the Fantasy label, which released *San Francisco '83* and *I'm in A Phone Booth, Baby,* two blues classics. King performed at the Filmore West Concert in 1968, where he stole the show. After this performance King was named, "The most-imitated blues guitarist in the world." He was one of the first rhythm and blues singers to play with a symphony, when he recorded with the St. Louis Symphony and brought together blues and classical music.

In 1983, King was inducted into the W. C. Handy International Blues Awards Hall of Fame. In 1984, he won two Grammy nominations for his songs, *San Francisco '83* and *I'm in A Phone Booth, Baby*. He was also inducted into the Blues Foundation Hall of Fame in 1983.

His albums include the *Big Blues* in

1962, *Born Under a Bad Sign* in 1967, *Tomato Years* in 1976, *The Best of Albert King* in 1986, and *The Ultimate Collection* in 1993. King died of a heart attack on December 21, 1992, in Memphis.

Dorothy Moore, a native of Jackson, was born on October 13, 1947. Dorothy was raised by her great-grandmother and her singing talent was discovered at an early age. At age three, she had a vibrato in her voice and, as a result, she was given musical instruments and taken to gospel programs.

Moore began singing with The New Stranger Home Baptist Church Choir at age five and later became a soloist. She sang at the Alamo Theater talent shows, where she won first place many times.

Moore attended Smith Robinson Elementary School, Mary C. Jones Elementary, and Lanier High School in Jackson and later graduated from Jackson State University. While at Lanier High School, Dorothy won several talent shows.

After graduation from Lanier in 1965, Moore was discovered by a recording company producer in Jackson and in 1966, Moore signed with Epic Records. While attending Jackson State, she and two other students formed a female group called The Poppies. The Poppies worked with The Four Tops, Bobby Goldsboro, and Wilson Pickett. They recorded the hit singles *Lullaby of Love* and *He's Ready* for Columbia Records in 1966.

After performing with The Poppies, Moore went solo with Malaco Records in 1976. While at Malaco, she recorded the Grammy-nominated single, *Misty Blue*. Two years after *Misty Blue*, she recorded a second Grammy-nominated single, *I Believe You*. Moore has appeared on "Prime Time Country," "Nashville Now," "Ralph Emery," and other shows. In addition to the country and western and rhythm and blues recording sessions, Moore has also recorded numerous gospel songs.

Moore has earned four Grammy nominations, an Image Award, NATRA Female Rhythm and Blues Vocalist of the Year, *Billboard Magazine* Award, Governor's Award for Excellence in the Arts, and many other awards worldwide. Her single, *Misty Blue,* was used on the movie *Phenomenon* soundtrack.

Moore has appeared with such stars as Lou Rawls, Al Green, B. B. King, The Temptations, and others. She has also appeared on such shows as "American Bandstand," "Rock Concert," "Soul Train," and "The Midnight Special." She has recorded with several labels including Malaco, Volt, Rejoice, GSF, and Chimneyville.

Her albums include *Misty Blue* in 1976, *Once Moore With Feeling* in 1978, *Straight To You* in 1986, and *Feel the Love* in 1990. In addition, *Misty Blue and Other Great Hits* was released in 1997.

Brandy Rayanna Norwood was born February 11, 1979, in McComb where her father was a church music director. Norwood sang her first song in the

Brandy Norwood

church choir at the age of two. When Norwood was four, the family moved to Carson, California, but continued to maintain strong family ties in McComb.

In 1990, Norwood began participating in talent shows and charity events. At the age of eleven, she met a producer who took her to auditions with various record labels. She also sang back-up for Immature, a male trio. At fourteen, she signed with Atlantic Records. She began her career as a rhythm and blues "soul" singer at the age of fifteen.

Norwood recorded her first album, *Brandy*, released in 1994. This album made certified gold in just two months, and later triple platinum, selling more than three million copies. In 1996, Norwood won the Music Television Award for the Best Movie Song, *Sittin' Up In My Room*. She was also nominated for the Best New Artist Grammy Award in 1996 and won the 1996 Lady of Soul "Entertainer of the Year" Award. She also won the NAACP Image Award for Best New Artist, and the Soul Train Award for Best New Artist. Norwood recorded a duet with Lenny Kravitz, made a video with Boyz II Men, and was on the *Waiting To Exhale* soundtrack. Norwood has performed on "The Tonight Show" with Jay Leno. Norwood's second album, *Never Say Never*, was released in 1998. In 1999, this album was nominated for a Rhythm and Blues Grammy, and for the Record of the Year Grammy.

Norwood co-hosted the "American Music Awards" and was nominated for the Favorite Female Artist in the Pop and Rock category. Norwood received the nomination for the Favorite Female Artist in the Soul category. A big duo hit, *The Boy Is Mine*, was released with Monica in 1998. In 1999, this hit won the Best Rhythm and Blues Performance by a Duo or Group with Vocal Grammy.

Norwood has also begun an acting

career. In 1990, she appeared in *Arachnophobia* with a minor role. Three years later, she had a minor role in *Demolition Man*. Brandy's biggest acting success came in her own sitcom, "Moesha," which premiered in 1996. The next year, Norwood starred in the musical production of *Cinderella* and won the Image Award for Outstanding Youth Actor/Actress Award.

In 1998, Norwood was nominated for the Image Award for Outstanding Lead Actress in a Comedy Series for "Moesha," and she was also nominated for the Image Award for Outstanding Lead Actress in *Cinderella*. During 1998, Norwood had her first major role in a featured film, *I Still Know What You Did Last Summer,* and had a major role in the television movie with Diana Ross entitled "Double Platinum."

Today Norwood, her mother, father, and brother have their own company called Movin' On Productions to handle their touring and performances.

Her roots are still in McComb where Norwood's grandfather, Fred "Paw Paw" Bates, has several businesses.

Jimmy Reed was born Mathis James Reed in Dunleith on September 6, 1925, and stayed there until age fifteen. He learned harmonica and guitar from Eddie Taylor. Reed moved to Chicago in 1943 and served two years in the Navy. He became successful only after his third single *You Don't Have To Go* and *Boogie in the Dark*. He had blues and R&B record hits *Hush Hush, Big Boss Man,* and *Bright Lights, Big City*. He recorded fifty-six albums during his career and was inducted into the Rock and Roll Hall of Fame in 1991. His albums include *I'm Jimmy Reed* in 1956, *Just Jimmy Reed* in 1962, *Best of Jimmy Reed* in 1990, and *Speak the Lyrics to Me, Mama Reed* in 1993.

He died in Oakland, California, on August 29, 1976.

David Ruffin was born in Meridian on January 18, 1941. His family moved to Detroit where he and his brother Jimmy entered singing competitions. Ruffin began his musical career at Anna Records, and his first solo release was *I'm In Love/One Of These Days*. He followed up with two singles on another label, Check-Mate, that were written by rhythm and blues composer Billy Davis. He had hits during the 1960s like *My Girl, Ain't Too Proud To Beg, Beauty Is Only Skin Deep,* and *I Wish It Would Rain*.

Although Ruffin had the ability to remain a solo artist, he explored other areas of the music industry. He found an opportunity with Motown's premier male vocal group, The Temptations. The group had not realized any immediate success until their release with the first single Ruffin appeared on, *The Way You Do The Things You Do*.

The song quickly became a national hit and climbed to No. 11 on the charts. Ruffin's *My Girl* reached No. 1 and remained on the pop charts for the first three months of 1965.

The Temptations had major hits in 1967 and 1968 with Ruffin as lead

David Ruffin

singer. He became one of the greatest lead singers Motown ever had.

In 1968, Ruffin left The Temptations to start a solo career. His first release, *My Whole World Ended*, reached the Top 10. He would have another Top 10 solo hit in late 1975 with his song *Walk Away From Love*. Two other singles, *Heavy Love* and *Everything Is Coming Up Love*, made the Top 10 on the rhythm and blues charts.

Motown released one album each year for Ruffin during the 1970s until the singer left for Warner Brothers. In 1982, Ruffin rejoined The Temptations for their reunion tour and album.

In May of 1985, Daryl Hall and John Oates invited Ruffin and Eddie Kendricks to join them at a benefit concert for the United Negro College Fund in Harlem's newly renovated Apollo Theater. That reunion resulted in a *Live at the Apollo* single and album. In 1988, RCA released the album entitled *Ruffin and Kendrick*. Ruffin can be heard on singles like *I'm In Love* (1961), *My Whole World Ended* (1969), *Heavy Love* (1976), *Still In Love With You* (1980), and *I Get Excited* (1979).

By 1989, Ruffin, Kendrick, and former Temptations lead singer Dennis Edwards were performing together on a regular basis. In June of 1991, the three had just returned to Philadelphia from a month-long tour of England when Ruffin died of a drug overdose.

Jimmy Ruffin, born in Collinsville on May 7, 1939, is the older brother of David Ruffin. As kids, David and Jimmy began their career with a gospel group called the Dixie Nightingales and signed with Anna Records. In 1964, the two brothers joined The Temptations. Jimmy Ruffin enjoyed several huge hits himself in the mid-1960s on the Soul Record label. Ruffin first signed with another Motown subsidiary, the short-lived Miracle, in 1961. He had a hit, *What*

Becomes of the Brokenhearted, that made him a star in 1966. He followed with *I've Passed This Way Before* and *Gonna Give Her All the Love I've Got.*

Following the release of the first album, the Ruffin brothers switched to another Detroit label, Check-Mate, where they produced two singles. Jimmy Ruffin was soon drafted into the Armed Forces. After his release, he went back to Motown to record for the Soul label in 1964.

In 1970, he briefly teamed with David as the Ruffin Brothers and cut a duet, *Stand by Me.* He also staged a comeback in 1980 on RSO Records with a major pop hit, *Hold On to My Love.*

His albums include *Sings Top 10* for Motown in 1966, *Jimmy Ruffin Way* for Motown in 1997, *Groove Governor* for Soul in 1970, and *Sunrise* for RSO in 1980.

Rufus Thomas was born on March 26, 1917, in Cayce. Soon after Thomas' family moved to Memphis, he began singing while he attended Booker T. Washington High School. At the age of thirteen, he worked as a master of ceremonies at amateur shows in the Palace Theater on Beale Street.

He also worked as a comic in numerous vaudevillian traveling entertainment troupes in the mid-1930s such as the Rabbit Foot Minstrels Show, the Georgia Dixon Traveling Show, and the Royal American Tent Shows. The likable Thomas returned to Memphis and formed a popular tap dance/scat singing act with Robert Counce, which was known as "Rufus and Bones."

He hosted amateur shows at the Palace and Handy theaters and replaced B. B. King as a deejay at WDIA, a black-owned radio station. In the early 1940s, he began to write blues and made his first recordings.

In 1951, Thomas started recording for Sam Phillips at the Memphis Recording Service. His first real success was the big hit *Bear Cat* which was Sun Records' first national hit in 1953. Several months later, he teamed up with guitarist Joe Hill Louis and recorded *Tiger Man.* Until the late 1970s, Thomas traveled overseas touring in England and Germany as well as doing television shows. The group Con Funk Shun featured Thomas at its 1973 Wattstax concert at the Los Angeles Forum. Thomas later joined Satellite with his daughter, Carla, in 1960, remaining there until the recording company became Stax a year later.

Thomas stayed at Stax until the company collapsed in 1975. He was successful in the 1970s with Southern Funk and recorded *Do the Funky Chicken, Do the Push and Pull,* and *The Breakdown.* All three songs

Rufus Thomas

made it to the rhythm and blues Top 5. While in the music business, Thomas has received several awards, including three lifetime achievement awards—one from Wings of Change, one from the Beale Street Merchants Association, and the first ever given by ASCAP. He also received the W. C. Handy Howlin' Wolf Award at the Chicago Blues Festival for Outstanding Blues Performance.

Thomas has flown to Poretta, Italy, to perform at the annual Soul Festival held in his honor at Rufus Thomas Park. He was also honored by the city of Memphis, which named a street for him.

Ike Turner was born in Clarksdale on November 5, 1931. At age eleven, Turner was back-up pianist for bluesman Sonny Boy Williamson. He co-wrote, with Delta bluesman James Cotton, what was probably the first rock and roll hit, *Rocket 88,* and backed Jackie Brenson on the record in 1951. He later formed the group Ike and Tina Turner in 1957. Ike and Tina were married from 1958 to 1976. Much of Turner's musical influence came from the Mississippi Delta and can be heard in his powerful renditions of songs such as *A Fool in Love, I Idolize You, Poor Fool,* and *Tra La La La.*

In 1960, he developed a dynamic stage show around Tina. Their biggest hit record was the Top 5 million-seller *Proud Mary* (No. 4 in 1971). Their many hits include *It's Gonna Work Out Fine, River Deep, Mountain High, I Want to Take You Higher,* and *Nutbush City Limits.* Ike released eighty-seven albums with Tina and fourteen solo albums. Ike and Tina were inducted into the Rock and Roll Hall of Fame in 1991.

Rock and Roll

.....

Rock and roll is another form of music with roots in Mississippi. The first true rock and roll recording was done by Jackie Brenson, who was born in Clarksdale.

    Everyone is familiar with how Elvis Presley listened to and played with black musicians, which led to him developing his own unique and popular form of rock and roll.

    In addition, Mississippi produced many college and "garage rock" bands in the 1950s and 1960s. Several examples of these bands appear in this chapter.

Andy Anderson and the Rolling Stones. Andy Anderson was born in Jackson about 1935. Anderson was a rock and roll singer and musician who formed a group called "The Rolling Stones" in Starkville in 1955, long before the famous British group took that name. Members of the band were Joe Tubb on lead guitar, "Cuz" Covington on bass, Roy Estes on piano, Bobby Lyons on drums, and Andy Anderson as lead singer.

The group even recorded on London Records, the same label used by the famous Stones. The Mississippi "Stones" had the first rock record in history to be distributed worldwide, *Johnny Valentine*. The record sold more than 600,000 copies.

Their song, *You Shake a Me Up*, was one of the few songs in history to become the Pick of the Week in *Cashbox, Billboard,* and *Music Reporter* all in the same week.

> • • • • •
> ### Mississippi First:
> THE FIRST ROLLING STONES ROCK GROUP WAS FROM MISSISSIPPI. BEFORE THE MORE FAMOUS GROUP FROM ENGLAND, ANDY ANDERSON AND THE ROLLING STONES WERE RECORDING UNDER THAT NAME AND, IRONICALLY, BY THE SAME RECORDING COMPANY AS THE OTHER ROLLING STONES.
> • • • • •

The Rolling Stones appeared on Dick Clark's "American Bandstand," "Wink Martindale's Dance Party," and "Teen Tempos."

The band dissolved in 1959 with members taking up various other careers.

Andy Anderson and the Rolling Stones

Blind Melon is a hard-rock group of six that included three Mississippians. They are Glen Graham, drummer, born in Columbus on December 5, 1967; Brad Smith, bass guitarist, born in Columbus on September 29, 1968; and Thomas Roger Stevens, guitarist, born in West Point on October 31, 1969.

The group was featured on a cover photo (nude), on the November 11, 1993, issue of *Rolling Stone Magazine*. Their first album in 1993, *Blind Melon*, went double platinum with a hit single and video from the album called *No Rain*. Their second album, *Soup*, was released in August 1995.

Their third album, *Nico*, was released in November of 1996 after the death of their lead singer.

Delaney Bramlett was born in Pontotoc County on July 1, 1939. He moved to Los Angeles in the 1960s where he appeared on the TV show "Shindig." He had hit single records, *Only You Know and I Know* (No. 20 in 1971) with the rock and roll group "Delaney & Bonnie" (Bonnie was his wife) and *Never Ending Song of Love* (No. 13 in 1971) as "Delaney & Bonnie & Friends." The friends were backup artists, making up a "Who's Who" of rock music, and included Eric Clapton, Duane Allman, Rita Coolidge, Dave Mason, Leon Russell, Jim Gordon, and others.

Clapton, Gordon, and some of the other friends formed Derek and the Dominoes after performing together on Delaney & Bonnie's 1969-70 tour. Clapton's later style was heavily influenced by the time he spent with Delaney & Bonnie.

Bramlett recorded a total of sixteen albums with his wife, Bonnie Lynn, who was born in Pontotoc County on November 11, 1944, and "friends."

Delaney & Bonnie dissolved their marriage and the group in 1972.

Bramlett's albums include *To Bonnie From Delaney* in 1970 on Atco, *Motel Shot* in 1971 on Atco, *Something's Coming* in 1972 on Columbia, and *Together* in 1972 on CBS. He also had several solo albums including *Mobius Trip* for CBS.

> **Mississippi First:**
> JACKIE BRENSON, BORN IN CLARKSDALE, RECORDED THE FIRST TRUE ROCK AND ROLL RECORD, *ROCKET 88*.

Jackie Brenson was born in Clarksdale on August 15, 1930. He had a No. 1 hit record, *Rocket 88* (1951), that is considered by many to be the first true rock and roll record. The song was co-written by two other Mississippians, Ike Turner, who played with Brenson on the record, and Delta bluesman James Cotton. Brenson died December 15, 1979.

(See also Blues)

Jimmy Buffett was born on December 25, 1946, in Pascagoula. The son of a naval architect, he was raised in Mobile, Alabama in the 1950s and 1960s. Buffett attended Catholic schools in his elementary and high school years, then graduated from the University of Southern Mississippi in 1969. While at USM

Jimmy Buffett

majoring in history and journalism, he was drawn to the music scene of New Orleans, and performed in local night clubs where he developed his fun, irreverent, and laid-back style.

Buffett's experiences in New Orleans encouraged him toward a musical career. Buffett moved to Nashville, where he found a job writing for *Billboard Magazine,* further developing his skills as a writer. He got a recording contract with Barnaby Records and in 1970, recorded his first album, *Down to Earth.*

Down to Earth was a country-style album, which failed to earn Buffett any musical recognition. Buffett then worked as a singer in Florida and the Caribbean without much success.

In 1973, Buffett relocated again, this time to Los Angeles. Los Angeles held many distractions for him which did not serve his career, so he decided to return to Key West, Florida. ABC released his *A White Sport Coat and a Pink Crustacean* in 1973 and *Living and Dying in 3/4 Time* in 1974, again without much success.

Buffett felt that Key West was the place where he could best promote his tropical folk-rock style of music, which is a blend of folk, rock, and country music. Buffett's next two albums were more successful. He also appeared in the motion picture *Rancho Deluxe.*

By 1975, Buffett had organized his own band, known as the Coral Reefer Band, that included his old friend from college, Greg "Fingers" Taylor.

Although Buffett's success was beginning to climb, one song launched him into stardom. It was his Top 10 chart-topping single, *Margaritaville,* in 1977. This song enabled his album *Changes in Attitudes, Changes in Latitudes* to become his first platinum recording.

In addition to his talents as a musician, Buffett is also a writer. He has written three books, two of which have been bestsellers: *Tales from Margaritaville: Fictional Facts and Factual Fiction* and *Where is Joe Merchant?* This book spent twenty-seven weeks on the *New York Times* bestseller list. He has also written *A Pirate Looks at Fifty, The Jolly Mon,* and *Trouble Dolls.*

His "Parrothead" fan clubs have sprung up all over the world. His followers are present whenever he performs on the "Today Show" on NBC and at sold-out concerts. According to *Fortune* magazine, he is one of the highest paid entertainers in the United States. For example, he was in the top forty highest paid entertainers in 1995, with $26 million in earnings. He has expanded into clothing, night clubs, and literature.

He was recently inducted into the Mississippi Musicians Hall of Fame.

Jerry Butler, born in Sunflower County on December 8, 1939, moved to Chicago at the age of three. Butler's music lessons as a young boy came in the church choir. With friends from the choir, he formed the R&B group, The Roosters. This group eventually became Jerry Butler and the Impressions.

Butler became one of the biggest rock and roll and soul singers of all time. He was dubbed "The Iceman" because of his cool delivery while singing on stage. Butler and the Impressions' biggest gold-selling hit records were *For Your Precious Love* (No. 11 in 1958), *He Will Break Your Heart* (No. 7 in 1960), and *Only the Strong Survive* (No. 4 million-seller in 1969). Several other hits included *Moon River, Hey, Western Union Man,* and *Let It Be Me,* a Top-5 hit record duo with Betty Everett (from Greenwood). He recorded more than sixty-two albums.

Ace Cannon was born on May 5, 1934, in Grenada. He began to play alto saxophone at the age of ten and recorded with Sun Records during the early days of rock and roll. He developed into one of Nashville's most successful session men in the late 1950s through the early 1970s. Sam Phillips of Sun Records said, "Ace Cannon is the greatest saxophone player who ever lived." Cannon has since been dubbed the "Godfather of Sax."

In 1959, he joined the Bill Black Combo and recorded for the Hi label. The combo appeared on popular TV shows of the time, including "The Ed Sullivan Show," "The Merv Griffin Show," and "American Bandstand."

In 1962, Cannon made his first solo recording, *Tuff,* an instrumental which made the Top 20 on the country music charts. Next, his *Blues Stay Away from Me* made it into the Top 40. He had two more hits in the 1960s with *Cottonfields* and *Searchin',* recorded on Hi. After moving to Nashville in the 1970s, Cannon had a minor hit, *Blue Eyes Crying in the Rain,* and he received a nomination for the Best Country Instrumental Performance Grammy that year.

In 1986, Cannon performed on *The Class of '55* album which brought together Jerry Lee Lewis, Carl Perkins, Johnny Cash and Roy Orbison for the first time. This led to Cannon and Perkins pairing up for a tour which lasted the entire year.

His recordings include *Ace in the Hole, Ace of Sax, Aces High, Cool and Saxy,* and *Country Cannon.*

The Gants were one of the few garage bands from the Deep South to make a national name in the 1960s. The Greenwood pop band hit the Top 50 in 1965 with *Roadrunner.* Their music was

The Gants, c. 1965.

a blend of mid-tempo acoustic and electric guitars, close harmonies, and a bit of country.

The members were Don Wood on drums, Sid Herring on vocals and guitar, John Sanders on rhythm guitar, and Vince Montgomery on bass.

Their albums include *Roadrunner* in 1965 for Liberty, *Gants Galore* in 1966 for Liberty, and *Gants Again* in 1966 also for Liberty. Although the group never had another hit after *Roadrunner*, they still keep trying with reunions, a 2000 release of *The Best of the Gants* album by Sundazed, and some sessions on weekends.

The members have all taken different careers since they were a group thirty years ago. A lawyer, obstetrician and several businessmen represent those careers. John Sanders says that their music now is purely recreational.

Jerry Lee Lewis was born near Ferriday, Louisiana, in 1935. However, he has been a long-time resident of Nesbit, Mississippi, where he owns a ranch.

When he was five, his talent on the piano was noticed by his parents, Elmo and Mamie Lewis. They realized that he was born with a natural talent and mortgaged their home to buy young Lewis a piano.

At the age of fifteen, Lewis began to perform with a traveling tent revival. He enrolled in the Texas Bible Institute after graduating from high school, but was expelled after playing a boogie-woogie version of a hymn.

At the age of twenty-two, he and his father gathered and sold thirty dozen eggs to pay for a trip to Memphis where Lewis would meet with Sam Phillips and sign with Sun Records.

Despite upsets in his personal life, Lewis kept performing and launched his biggest hit ever, *Great Balls of Fire*. For a while, he found himself blacklisted on radio and television because of his lifestyle.

His many albums include *Jerry Lee Lewis* in 1975 on Rhino, *The Killer Rocks* in 1972 on Mercury, *Live at the Star Club* in 1980 on Rhino, and *Rockin' My Life Away* in 1991 on Tomato. In 1986, he was the first artist to be inducted into the

Rock and Roll Hall of Fame. The movie *Great Balls of Fire,* a profile of his life, was made in the same year. In 1993, he wrote and published his autobiography, *Killer.* In early April of 1996, he was named a Professor of Rock and Roll by the University of Memphis.

His 1997 tour covered parts of Europe and Moscow. He has recorded more than 1,200 songs.

Elvis Aaron Presley was born in Tupelo on January 8, 1935, and grew up on Old Saltillo Road in Tupelo until age thirteen. He later legally changed his middle name to Aron. On his eleventh birthday, Presley received his first guitar which cost $12.75. Presley loved gospel music and sang in a Pentecostal church choir, where he developed his singing talents. He was influenced by another Mississippi group, the Blackwood Brothers. He performed with small bands around the South for school dances when school administrators would permit. He was turned down many times because of his gyrations on stage.

In 1948, Presley and his family moved to Memphis, where he attended Humes High School. This is where Presley grew his hair long and greased it back. He also grew long sideburns and wore flashy clothes.

Presley's recording career started in 1953 when he went to a recording studio in Memphis, Sun Records, to record two songs for his

Jerry Lee Lewis

Elvis Presley, the King of Rock and Roll, c. 1973.

mother's birthday present. Sam Phillips, the owner of Sun Records, wasn't impressed with Presley's singing.

Finally, in July of 1954, Phillips recognized Presley's potential as he sang *That's Alright Mama*. In 1956, Presley met Colonel Tom Parker, who became his manager and helped him with his first hit, *Heartbreak Hotel*. Following this major hit were songs like *Hound Dog, All Shook Up, Don't Be Cruel,* and *Burning Love,* all hits in the same year.

Presley then starred in his first motion picture, *Love Me Tender,* in 1956. The U.S. Army drafted him and he served

·····
Mississippi First:
ELVIS PRESLEY, BORN IN TUPELO, WAS FIRST AS THE "KING OF ROCK AND ROLL."
·····

two years. When Presley was discharged from the Army, he released *Are You Lonesome Tonight,* which stayed at the top of the charts for four weeks. He will also be remembered for *Blue Suede Shoes, Jailhouse Rock, Always on My Mind, Your Cheatin' Heart, Don't be Cruel,* and many more. Presley married Priscilla Beaulieu, on May 1, 1967, at the Alldin Hotel, in Las Vegas.

Presley died August 16, 1977. Because of his influence, rock and roll music rose to new levels.

Presley was recently inducted into the Mississippi Musicians Hall of Fame.

Greg "Fingers" Taylor is a native of Kansas but moved to Jackson when he was in high school; Jackson has been home ever since. He got his stage name during his early years in the music business in Jackson. His fans named him "Fingers" after hearing him play piano one night at a high school dance.

He was influenced by rock and soul music in the 1950s and 1960s, and it was during that time that he started playing the harmonica as his primary instrument. He liked the idea of carrying his instrument in his pocket.

In 1970, while a student at the University of Southern Mississippi, he was invited to join the Nitty Gritty Dirt Band on stage during a concert.

The then-unknown singer and songwriter Jimmy Buffett came to Southern, and Taylor and Buffett got together for a jam session. That event, formed in 1971, forged a relationship that still endures today.

In 1971, Taylor joined Larry Raspberry and the Highsteppers, a rhythm and blues band out of Memphis. He stayed with that group for three-and-a-half years. On tour in a series of one-nighters, the group signed with Stax Records and recorded an album called *Highstepping and Fancy Dancing*.

During that time, he played backup with several artists, including Jerry Lee Lewis. He also recorded with Buffett, who had signed with ABC Records.

Taylor's harmonica became a feature of Buffett's sound, and he was a founding member of Buffett's "Coral Reefer Band" in 1975. Consequently, he moved to Nashville and went on tour with Buffett.

That group toured all during the 1970s and 1980s. In the 1990s, the band became a major concert draw with a "cult" following. Buffett has given due credit to Taylor for his contribution to the Coral Reefer Band.

However, Taylor was working on his own career and in 1984 produced his first solo album, *Harpoon Man*. It was released on the English label Red Lightnin'. His second album, *Chest Pains*, is a collection spotlighting his vocal and instrumental work. He recorded several other albums for release in the U.S. and Europe. One of these is *New Fingerprints*, released in 1993.

More recently he has formed his own group but still tours and plays concerts as part of Buffett's organization. He continues to write new music and develop new styles of performing.

Mary Wilson was born in Greenville on March 6, 1944. Her family moved to Detroit when she was three. However, she continued to visit her grandparents in Mississippi during the summer.

She is a founding member of The Supremes, one of the most famous vocal groups in musical history. She was with The Supremes for thirteen years and during that time traveled the world extensively. She has written two best-selling autobiographies and released her own solo disc, *Walk The Line*.

Wilson and The Supremes signed with Motown Records in 1963. They are known for such songs as *Where Did Our Love Go, Baby Love, Come See About Me,* and *Stop In The Name Of Love*. The music of The Supremes crossed racial and cultural barriers.

After Diana Ross left the group in 1970 to pursue a solo career, Wilson stayed on and the group had four million-selling albums. The band continued until 1977, recording hits like *Up The Ladder to the Roof, Stoned Love, Floy Joy,* and *Everybody's Got the Right To Love*.

Motown released two albums with Wilson as soloist, *Mary Wilson* in 1979 and *Red Hot* in 1979. In addition, CEO released an album featuring Wilson entitled *Walk the Line*. She can be heard on the 1991 release *'70s Greatest Hits and Rare Classics* by The Supremes.

Wilson has written two best-selling autobiographies, *Dreamgirl: My Life as a Supreme* and *Supreme Faith*.

Mississippi Music Heritage Museum

Efforts are underway by the Mississippi Musicians Hall of Fame Board to fund and build a Mississippi Music Heritage Museum. This museum will, first, show how American music was born in Mississippi, and second, allow visitors to have an actual musical experience through singing and playing musical instruments. Visitors will move through diorama rooms related to the state's musical history in blues, gospel, country, and other genres.

The museum has been endorsed by such world-famous Mississippi musicians as Leontyne Price, opera singer and James Blackwood, gospel singer. The museum will have national significance because it will preserve and showcase how America's music was born and the musicians who made it possible.

References

All Music Guide internet web site <http://allmusic.com>

Baker, Robert M., *A Brief History of the Blues*, [on-line] Available: http://www.thebluehighway.com/history.html, 2000

Barton, Dee, Interviewed by Jim Brewer, 1997

Berendt, Joachim E., *The Jazz Book: From Ragtime to Fusion and Beyond*, Lawrence Hill Books, Brooklyn, New York, 1992 (rev. 1997)

Bishop, Edward Allen, *Elsie McWilliams - I Remember Jimmie*, self published by Allen Bishop, Meridian, MS 1985

Blackwood, James, With Dan Martin, *The James Blackwood Story*, Whitaker House, Monroeville, PA, 1975

Bownam, Rob, *Malaco Records: The Last Soul Company*, self published Malaco Records, 1999

Brown, Ashley, Editor, *Popular Music, Vol. 1-20*, Marshall Cavendish Publisher

Clarke, Donald, *Penguin Encyclopedia of Pop Music*, London, 1989

Cooper, Forrest Lamar, *Mississippi Trivia IV*, printed by EverGreen Press, Jackson, MS, 1990

Cox, James L., *Mississippi Almanac*, Lithographed by Rose Printing Company, Tallahassee, FL, 1995

Cox, James L., *Mississippi Almanac 1997-1998*, Lithography by Rose Printing Company, Tallahassee, Fl, 1997

Dennis, Perry Jr., *Four Pioneer Mississippi Bandmasters, and A History of The Mississippi Bandmasters Association*, self published, 1985

Dickerson, James L.,*Country Music's Most Embarrassing Moments*, Guild Bindery Press, Germantown, TN, 1996

Dickerson, James, *Goin' Back To Memphis*, Schirmer Books, New York, N.Y., 1996

Dickerson, James, *That's Alright, Elvis*, Simon & Schuster Macmillan, New York, N.Y., 1997

Dickerson, James, *Women On Top - The Quiet Revolution That Is Rocking The Music Industry*, Billboard Books, New York, N.Y. 1998

Erlewin, Michael, Vladimir Bogdanov, Chris Woodstra and Cub Coda, *All Music Guide to the Blues*, Miller Freeman Books, San Francisco, 1996

Feather, Leonard, *The Encyclopedia of Jazz*, New York, Harizon Press, 1966

Ferris, William, *Blues From the Delta*, Da Capo Press, N.Y., 1979

Frew, Timothy, *Elvis*, Mallard Press, New York, N.Y., 1992

Gottlieb, William P., *The Golden Age Of Jazz*, Pomegranet Artbooks, San Francisco, CA, 1995

Gourse, Leslie, *Madam Jazz*, Oxford University Press, MS

Griffith, Paul, *The Thames and Hudson Encyclopedia of 20-Century* Music, Thames and Hudson, London, New York, 1986

Handy, D. Antoinette, *Black Conductors*, The Scarecrow Press, Metuchen, NJ and London, England, 1995

Handy, D. Antoinette, *The International Sweethearts of Rhythm*, The Scarecrow Press, Metuchen, N.J. and London, England, 1983

Handy, D. Antoinette, *The International Sweethearts of Rhythm*, Revised Edition, The Scarecrow Press, Lanham, MD and London, 1998

Handy, W. C., *Father of the Blues, an Autobiography*, Da Capo Press, New York, N. Y., 1941

Harris, Sheldon, *Blues Who's Who: A Biographical Dictionary of Blues Singers*, New Rochelle, NY, Arlington House, 1979

Harris, Sheldon, *Blues Who's Who*, Da Capo Press, New York, N.Y.,1970

Internet web sites of various Mississippi musicians

LaBlanc, Michael, Editor, *Contemporary Musicians -Vol. 1-27*, Gale Research Inc., Detroit, 1989

Larkin, Colin, ed. *The Guinness Encyclopedia of Popular Music*. Volume 1. New York: Guinness Publishing, 1995

Lee, William F., Stan Kenton, *Artistry in Rhythm*, Creative Press, Los Angeles, California, 1984

Lomax, Alan, *The Land Where The Blues Began*, Pantheon Books, New York, N.Y.,1993

Lowe, Mundell, Interviewed by Jim Brewer, 1998

Malone, Bill C., *Country Music USA: A Fifty-Year History*, Austin, TX, University of Texas Press, 1968

Malone, Bill C., *Southern Music American Music*, The University Press Of Kentucky, Lexington, KY, 1979

McWilliams, Skeets, Interviewed by Jim Brewer, 1998

Mississippi Writers and Musicians Project of Starkville High School, Internet web site<http://SHS.Starkville.K12.MS.US/mswm/MSWritersAndMusicians/musicians>

Palmer, Robert, *Deep Blues*, Penguin Books, New York, N.Y.,1981

Pareles, John and Patricia Romanowski, *The Rolling Stone Encyclopedia of Rock and Roll*, New York Press, 1983

Pride, Charley and Henderson, Jim, *Pride, The Charley Pride Story*, William Morrow & Company, New York, N.Y., 1994

Racine, Kree Jack, *Above All (Lives And Careers of the Blackwood Brothers)*, Jarodoce Publications, Memphis, TN, 1967

Ryan, Marc, *Trumpet Records, An Illustrated History With Discography*, Big Nickel Publications, Milford New Hampshire, 1992

Sedie, Stanley, Editor, *The New Grove Dictionary of Music and Musicians,* Vol. 1-20, Macmillian Publishers, London, Washington D.C., 1980

Sales, Grover, *Jazz: America's Classical Music,* Englewood Cliffs, N.J., Prentice Hall, 1984

Stambler, Irwin, *Encyclopedia of Pop, Rock, and Soul, Revised Edition,* New York, St. Martin's Press, 1989

Vinton, John, *Directory of Contemporary Music,* E. P. Dutton, New York, 1974

Wardlow, Gale Dean, *Chasin' That Devil Music, Searching for the Blues,* San Francisco, Miller Freeman (Backbeat) Books, 1998

Weaver, David, *Ruby Elzy (1908-1943)* [on-line]. Available: http://www.afrovoices.com/elzy.html, 2000. Weaver, author of the forthcoming biography, *Ain't Got Long to Stay Here: The Ruby Elzy Story,* is the contributor of the Ruby Elzy article and has devoted more than two years researching the life and career of Ruby Elzy. Weaver's career in the performing arts and public broadcasting spans more than 20 years. He lives in Columbus, Ohio.

Wilson, Christine, *All Shook Up, Mississippi Roots Of American Popular Music,* Mississippi Department of Archives And History, Jackson, MS, 1995

Workman, Nanette, *Nanette Workman, a Biography,* Les Editions Internationales Alain Stanke, Montreal Quebec, 1999 (Published in French)

Resources

BOOKS

Arvey, Vema. *In One Lifetime* (William Grant Still). University of Arkansas Press, 1984. MS B S857

Barclay, Pamela. *Charley Pride.* Creative Education, 1974, cl975. MS JB P947

The Best of Tammy Wynette. Warner Bros., [1982]. MS 784.52 W985

Broonzy, Big Bill. *Big Bill Blues.* Da Capo Press, 1992. MS B B873

Brown, Peter. *Down at the End of Lonely Street: The Life and Death of Elvis Presley.* Dutton, 1997. MS B P934

Buffett, Jimmy. *A Pirate Looks at Fifty.* Random House, 1998. MS B B929

Calt, Stephen. *King of the Delta Blues: The Life and Music of Charlie Patton.* Rock Chapel Press, 1988. MS B P322

Catalano, Grace. *LeAnn Rimes: Teen Country Queen.* Dell Publishing, 1997. MS B R575

Charters, Samuel Barclay. *The Bluesmen: The Story and the Music of the Men Who Made the Blues.* Oak Publications, [1967-77].781.643 MS C486 v. 1

Coffey, Frank. *The Complete Idiot's Guide to Elvis.* Alpha Books, 1997. MS B P934

Cross, Wilbur. *The Conway Twitty Story: An Authorized Biography.* Doubleday, 1986. MS B T972

Danchin, Sebastian. *Blues Boy: The Life and Music of B. B. King.* University Press of Mississippi, 1998. MS BK52

Dennis, Allen. *James Blackwood Memories.* Quail Ridge Press, 1997. MS B B632

DeWitt, Howard. *Elvis, the Sun Years: The Story of Elvis Presley in the Fifties.* Popular Culture, 1993. MS B P934

Dixon, Willie. *I Am the Blues: The Willie Dixon Story.* Da Capo Press, 1989. MS BD621

Dundy, Elaine. *Elvis and Gladys.* Macmillan, 1985. MS B P934

Early, Donna Presley. *Elvis: Precious Memories.* Best of Times, 1997. MS B P934

Edwards, Honeyboy. *The World Don't Owe Me Nothing: The Life and Times of Delta Bluesman Honeyboy Edwards.* Chicago Review Press, 1997. MS B E26

Elvis: His Life in Pictures. Abbeville Publishing Group, 1997. MS B P934

Eng, Steve. *Jimmy Buffett: The Man from Margaritaville Revealed.* St. Martin's Press, 1996. MS B B929

Esposito, Joe. *Good Rockin' Tonight: Twenty Years on the Road and on the Town with Elvis.* Simon & Schuster, 1994. MS B P934

Ferris, William. *Blues from the Delta.* Da Capo, 1984. MS 781.643 F394 1984

Geller, Larry. *If I Can Dream: Elvis' Own Story.* Simon and Schuster, 1989. MS B P934

Gentry, Bobbie. *Bobbie Gentry Songbook.* Larry Shayne Music, 1967. MS 784.4 G339

Gentry, Bobbie. *Patchwork.* Larry Shayne Music, 1971. MS 784.4 G339

Greenwood, Earl. *The Boy Who Would Be King: An Intimate Portrait of Elvis Presley.* Dutton Book, 1990. MS B P934

Gregory, Neal. *When Elvis Died.* Communications Press, 1980. MS B P934

Guralnick, Peter. *Careless Love: The Unmaking of Elvis Presley.* Little, Brown, 1999. MS B P934

Guralnick, Peter. *Searching for Robert Johnson.* Dutton, 1989. MS B J68

Haining, Peter. *Elvis in Private.* Chivers Press, 1987. LP MS B P934

Handy, W. C. *Father of the Blues: An Autobiography.* Da Capo Press, 1991. MS B H236

Heard, Dick. *Elvis Up Close: In the Words of Those Who Knew Him Best.* Turner Pub., cl994.MS B P934

Humphrey, Mark. *The Jimmy Buffett Scrapbook*. Carol Pub. Group, c1993. MS B B929

King, B.B. *Blues All Around Me: The Autobiography of B. B. King*. Avon Books, 1996. MS B K52

Kostelanetz, Richard. *The B. B. King Companion: Five Decades of Commentary*. Schirmer Books, 1997. MS 781.643 B658

Krishef, Robert. *Jimmie Rodgers*. Lerner Publications Co., 1978. MS JB R691

Lomax, Alan. *The Land Where the Blues Began*. Pantheon Books, 1993. MS 781.643 L839

Lyon, Hugh Lee. *Leontyne Price: Highlights of a Prima Donna*. Vantage Press, [1973]. MS B P945

Paris, Mike. *Jimmie the Kid:The Life of Jimmie Rodgers*. Da Capo Press, 1977. MS B R691 1981

Parker, John. *Elvis: The Secret Files*. Anaya, 1993. MS B P93

Porterfield, Nolan. *Jimmie Rodgers: The Life and Times of America's Blue Yodeler*. University of Illinois Press, 1992. MS B R691 1992

Pride, Charley. *Pride: The Charley Pride Story*. W. Morrow, 1994. MS B P947

Richardson, Jerry Scott. *The Blues Guitar Style of B. B. King*. UMI, 1987. MS 781.643 K52 1987

Rodgers, Carrie Cecil Williamson. *My Husband, Jimmie Rodgers*. Country Music Foundation Press, 1975. MS BR691 1975

Rodgers, Jimmie.. *The Legendary Jimmie Rodgers: Memorial Folio*. Peer International, 1967. MS 784.5206 R691 v. I

Rodman, Gilbert B. *Elvis After Elvis: The Posthumous Career of a Living Legend*. Rutledge, 1996. MS 781.66 P934

Ryan, Thomas. *The Parrot Head Companion: An Insider's Guide to Jimmy Buffett*. Carol Pub. Group, 1998. MS B B929

Sacre, Robert. *The Voice of the Delta: Charley Patton and the Mississippi Blues Traditions: Influences and Comparisons: An International Symposium*. Presses Universitaires Liege, 1987. MS 781.643 P322 1987

Sawyer, Charles. *The Arrival of B. B. King: The Authorized Biography*. Doubleday, 1980. MS B K52

Thibodeaux, Keith. *Life after Lucy: The True Story of Keith Thibodeaux - "I Love Lucy's" Little Ricky*. New Leaf Press, 1993. MS B T427

Weatherly, Jim. *The Songs of Jim Weatherly*. Keca Music, 1974. MS 784 . 3 W362

Whitmer, Peter. *The Inner Elvis: A Psychological Biography of Elvis Aron Presley*. Hyperion, 1996. MS 782!42166 P9

Wilson, Mary. *Supreme Faith: Someday We'll Be Together*. Harper Collins, 1990.MS B W751

Wilson, Shirley. *From Aaron Jenkins to Harold Jenkins: Conway Twitty's Roots*. Conway Twitty Enterprises, 1985. MS 929.2 J52

Wolff, Daniel. *You Send Me: The Life and Times of Sam Cooke*. W. Morrow, 1995. MS B C773

Wynette, Tammy. *Stand By Your Man*. Simon and Schuster, 1979. MS B W985

MEDIA

Almost Home: Living with Suffering and Dying (Sister Thea Bowman). Oblate Media and Communication Corporation, 1989. V2839, V2840

B. B. King, Blues Musician. Mississippi Center for Educational Television, 1977. VO178

B. B. King at Parchman Prison. Mississippi Authority for Educational Television, 1984. V0614

Big Joe: One More Time. Mississippi Center for Educational Television, 1983. V0619

Blues Maker (Fred McDowell). Center for the Study of Southern Culture, [198-?]. VI 903

Bluesmen. Mississippi Center for Educational Television, c 1977. VO180

Bowman, Thea. *Sister Thea: Songs of My People*. Krystal Records, 1988. PI39, P627

Bowman, Thea. *'Round the Glory Manger Christmas Spirituals*. Daughters of St. Paul, 1989. P623, P624

Elvis '68 Comeback Special. Music Media, 1984. V0422

Elvis: Aloha from Hawaii. Media Home Entertainment, 1984. V0407

Elvis: A Portrait by His Friends. New Image Studio, 1987. *Heart & Soul*, v. 1, V1676; *Untold Stories*, v.2, V1677 *The Fans*, v.3, VI 678; *A Perspective*, v.4, V 1679.

Elvis—One Night With You. Music Media, 1985. V0630

First Ladies of Opera (Leontyne Price). Video Artists International, cl988. V2063

Gershwin, George. *Great Scenes from Porgy and Bess* (Leontyne Price). RCA Victor, 1963.PHONODISC 0613

Land Where the Blues Began. Mississippi Authority for Educational Television, 1979. V0309

Leontyne Price Sings Noel. CBC Enterprises, 1987. VI 154

Mississippi, Music and Musicians. Mississippi Educational Television, 1983. V0239

Sam Chatmon: Sitting on Top of the World. Mississippi Authority for Educational Television, 1983. V0618

Sister Thea: Her Own Story. Oblate Media & Communication Corporation, 1991. V2391, V2392

Still, William Grant. *Piano Music*. William Still Music, 1988. Pl 17, P 1 18

The Mississippi Mass Choir. Malaco Video, 1989. V2332, V2333

William C. Handy: Father of the Blues. Llewellyn, 1975. K0172

Explanation of abbreviations: K=Kit; LP=Large Print; MS=Mississippi Collection; P=Phonotape; V=Video
Resources from the Mississippi Library Commission.
1221 Ellis Avenue • Jackson, Mississippi 39209 • E-mail: micref@mic.lib.ms.us • Webpage: http://www.mic.lib.ms.us
To borrow these or any other titles, contact your local library or call the Mississippi Library Commission toll free at 1-877-KWIK-REF or (601) 961-4111.

Index

Entries in bold face represent artists' profiles in the book or chapter opening pages.

•••••

A

A&R Records 65
ABC Records 30, 134, 160, 165
ABC-Paramount 82, 109
ABC/Dunhill 34, 90
Abdul, Paula 121
Abrams, Lawrence 90
Ace Music Publishers 138
Ace Records 34, 138
Acuff, Roy 37
Adelphi/Blue Horizon 21
Aerosmith 121
Akers, Garfield 14
Ala-Miss Records 138
Alabama 70
Albright, William 53
Alexander, John 44
Alexander, Texas 16
Alfred Publishing 50
Allen, Denise 30
Allen, Moses 109
Alligator Records 28, 34, 36, 39
Allison, Mose 98
Allman, Duane 24, 159
Alma Symphony 49
Aloisio, April 107
Altman, Robert 135
Amarillo Symphony 49
American Brass Quintet 47, 54
American Composers Orchestra 54
American Symphony 49
Ames, Roger 57
Ammons Publishing Co. 138
Ammons, Jimmie 138
Anderson, Andy, and the Rolling Stones 138, **158**
Anderson, Fay 106
Anderson, Lynne 67
Anderson, Marian 51
Anderson, Pete 63
Andre Previn Trio 122
Angel, Jimmy 139
Animals, The 22, 42, 149
Anka, Paul 106
Anna Records 153, 154
Anson and The Rockets 34
Anton, Susan 68
Arc Records 21
Argo Records 107
Arhoolie 17, 34
Arlen, Harold 46
Armstrong, Louis 98, 111
Arnold, Eddy 62, 71, 72
ARRA 61

Art Rupe Speciality Records 139
Atco Records 159
Atkins, Chet 62, 67, 73
Atlantic Records 38, 99, 113, 152
Atomic-H Records 17
Attache 132
Attaway, William 132
Atwood, Eden 107
Audiophile 103
Austin, Patti 120
Avanti Records 138, 139
Ayers, Roy 113

B

Bach, J. S. 47
Backstreet Boys 132
Bailey, Pearl 101, 106
Bailey, Phillip 24
Baker, Ginger 149
Baker, Jimmy 138
Baker, Ray 61
Baker, Robert M. 9
Ball, Earl Poole 60
Ballard, Glen 120
Baltimore Opera 44
Bandy, Marion "Moe" 61
Barber, Samuel 53
Bare, Bobby 72
Barlow, Wayne 48
Barnaby Records 160
Barnes, Roosevelt "Booba" 14, 140
Barrett, Bucky 61, 110
Barron, Kenny 113
Barry Goldberg Blues Band 34
Barry, Robert 102
Barrymore, Ethel 126
Bartok, Bela 99
Barton, Dee 121
Bartz, Gary 113
Bass, James Lansten "Lance" 132
Bass, Ralph 18
Bassett, Leslie 53
Bates, Otha Ellas 147
Beach Boys 134
Beaker Street 138
Beasley, Milton 138
Beatles, The 67, 78, 82
Beaulieu, Priscilla 165
Beck, Elder Charles 141
Beckett, Frederic Lee 99
Belafonte, Harry 132
Belew, Carl 72
Bell, Carey 141

Bellson, Louis 109
Ben Peters Music 71
Bennett, Betty 122
Bennett, Tony 122
Benson, George 120
Benton, Brook 150
Berendt, Joachim 10
Bernstein, Leonard 47
Berry, Chuck 104
Big Milton 31
Big Three Trio 19
Bill Black Combo 161
Bishop, Edward 10
Black Music Research Ensemble 44
Blackberry Records 95
Blackwood Brothers 11, 85, 86, **88**, 163
Blackwood, Doyle 88
Blackwood, James 11, **86**, 88
Blackwood, R. W. 88
Blackwood, Roy 88
Blailock, Steve 99, 110
Blakey, Art 102
Blakney, Andy 100
Bland, Bobby "Blue" 18, 24, 34, 139
Blind Melon 158
Blind Pig Records 36
Bloomfield, Mike 34
Blue Note 99, 102
Bluebird 21, 31, 41, 77
Blues 13
BMG 64, 132
BMG/RCA 53
BNA 79
Bobbin Records 32
Bobo, Willie 113
Bogdanovich, Peter 60
Bolcom, William 44
Bonds, Billy 139
Booker T. and the MGs 150
Boone, Pat 93
Boston Opera 44
Boston Pops, The 113
Boutte, Lillian 100
Bowie, Lester 101
Bowman, Rob 139
Boxcar Willie 62
Boyd, Edward Riley "Little Eddie" 14
Boys Choir of Harlem 57
Boyz II Men 152
Bracco, Lorraine 136
Bracey, Ishmon 10, **14**, 141
Bracy, Mississippi Coleman 141

Bradford, Bobby Lee 100
Bradley, Owen 138
Bramlett, Bonnie 159
Bramlett, Delaney 159
Brandy (see Norwood, Brandy)
Brenson, Jackie 14, 156, 157, **159**
Brevig, Per 47
Brim, John 150
Broadway 125
Bronson, Art 116
Brooklyn Philharmonic 44
Brookmeyer, Bobby 99
Brooks and Dunn 65
Broom Dusters, The 24
Broonzy, William Lee Conley "Big Bill" 15, 16, 19, 21
Brown, Army 107
Brown, James 110
Brown, Marion 112
Brown, Richard Jess 101
Brown, Ruth 104
Brown, Willie 23, 27, 35, 141
Brown, William 44
Brownlee, Archie 89
Brownlee, Leonard 93
Brunswick 141
Bryant, Roger, Jr. 90
Bryant, Bobby 101
Bryant, Ray 113
Buckaroos, The 60
Buckley, Tim 135
Buddah Records 104
Buffalo Philharmonic 49
Buffett, Jimmy 67, 70, **159**, 165
Bug/Capitol 20
Bullet Records 19
Bullock, Sandra 61
Bullseye Blues and Jazz 18
Burgh, Steve 64
Burks, James 90
Burnett, Chester Arthur "Howlin' Wolf" 15, 19, 20, 28, 34, 35, 39, 42
Burnside, R. L. 16
Burr, Gary 65
Burrell, Kenny 113
Burton, Wallace 107
Bush, Fred 50
Bush, President George 147
Butler, Jerry 161
Butler, Larry 60
Bychkov, Semyon 47
Byrd, D. 113
Byrds, The 135

C

C. F. Peters Publishing 54
Cadet Records 101
Cage, Nicolas 67
Callender, Red 102, 116
Callicott, Joe 14
Calloway, Cab 104, 111
Camail, John 60
Campanile Music Press 49
Campbell College Quartet 141
Campbell, Eddie 140
Campbell, Glen 72, 112
Campbell, Little Milton 24, 30, **31**, 138, 139
Cannon, Ace 161
Canton Spirituals 89, 138
Cantor, Eddie 106
Capitol Records 34, 38, 60, 102
Carl Fischer, Inc. 49
Carne, Jean 104
Carruthers, Earl 115
Carson, Johnny 23, 134
Carter, Benny 102, 104, 111, 115
Carter, Betty 99, 111
Carter, Bo 16, 32, 33, 141
Carter, John 100
Carter, President Jimmy 34, 126
Carter, Ron 123
Carter, Vicki Helms 126
Cash, Johnny 60, 79, 82, 161
Caston, Leonard "Baby Doo" 19
Cavett, Dick 106
CBS Records 80, 159
Centennial Records 50
Challenge Records 72
Chancellers, The 134
Chandler, Ben 93
Charlatans 134
Charles, Ray 62, 90, 149
Charly Records 15
Charter Nominees and Inductees 168
Chase, David 65
Chatmon Brothers, The 17
Chatmon, Armenter 16, 32
Chatmon, Lonnie 16, 32
Chatmon, Sam 16, 32, 33
Check-Mate Records 153, 155
Checker Chess label 42
Checker Records 32
Chenier, C. J. 24
Cher 136
Chess Records 15, 19, 38, 39
Chess/Checker Records 147
Chiao label 106
Chimneyville Records 151
Chon, Al 111
Choral Society of Greensboro 49
Christy, June 112
Cimmarons, The 81
Cincinnati Opera 44
Cincinnati Symphony 49, 54

Clapton, Eric 24, 25, 27, 38, 42, 98, 149, 150, 159
Clark, Dick 93, 158
Clark, Roger 64
Clash, The 98
Classical 43
Claud Blanchard Orchestra 111
Claude Thornhill Orchestra 111
Clayton, Willie 139
Clayton-Hamilton Jazz Orchestra 101
Clearwater, Eddy "The Chief" 17, 140
Cline, Patsy 62, 79
Clinton, President Bill 147
Clooney, Rosemary 72, 128
Cobb, Arnett 99
Cobra Records 38
Cochran Brothers, The 62
Cochran, Eddie 62
Cochran, Hank 60, **62**
Cohn, Al 117
Cole, Nat "King" 98, 107, 112, 116
Cole, Natalie 121
Coleman, J. P. 89
Coleman, Ornette 100
Coleman, Steve 115
Coley, Daryl 24
Collie, Shirley 62
Collins, Gary 128
Collins, Jamie Owens 93
Collins, Judy 135
Coltrane, John 102
Columbia Records 19, 23, 69, 72, 99, 103, 117, 141, 147, 151, 159
Commodore Records 117
Con Funk Shun 155
Conlee, John 71
Connick, Harry, Jr. 99
Contemporary Records 102
Continuum 47
Cooder, Ry 135
Cook, Peter 136
Cook, Samuel 146
Cooke, Dale 146
Cooke, L. C. 146
Cooke, Sam 146
Cool Cat Cannon 138
Coolidge, Rita 30, 112, 159
Coral Records 101
Coral Reefer Band 160, 166
Coronet Records 54
Cosby, Bill 37, 101
Costello, Elvis 98
Cotton Blossom Singers 90
Cotton Records 138
Cotton, James 15, **18**, 156, 159
Couch, Tommy 139
Counce, Robert 155
Count Basie 16, 101, 106, 115, 116
Country Music 59

Counts, Danny 64
Covington, Cuz 158
Crackerjacks 99, 138
Crawford, Hank 99
Crawford, Jimmie 109
Cray, Robert 150
Cream 25, 150
CRI 50
Crisler, Frank 90
Crosby, Bing 46, 106, 112
Crouch, Andrae 93, 112
Crudup, Arthur William "Big Boy" 18
Crumb, Earl 112
Crume, Rufus 93
Cryer, Sherwood 64
Cummings, Robert 102
Curry, Elder 141
Curtis, Peck 42
Cyrille, Andrew 113

D

Dakar label 146
Dalton, Kathy 135
Damone, Vic 101
Daniels, Charlie 62
Dardanelle Trio 103
Dave Clark 5, The 139
Davies, Ray 99
Davis, "Blind" John 19
Davis, Billy 153
Davis, Houston 138
Davis, Jimmie 112
Davis, Miles 104, 112, 115, 117
Davis, Paul 63
Davis, Skeeter 72
Davis, Tyrone 146
Debut Records 111
Decca Records 82
Dee Barton Orchestra 122
Dee, Kiki 120
Dee, Ruby 108
Delaney & Bonnie 159
Delmark 18, 19, 102, 113
Delos Records 54
Delta Records 138
Delta Rhythm Boys 101
Dennis, Benardo 19
DePriest, James 47
Derek and the Dominoes 159
Detroit Emeralds 103
Detroit Symphony 49, 54
Diamond Records 140
Dickens, Little Jimmy 62
Diddley, Bo 37, **147**
Dirty Looks 135
Divinyls 135
Dixie Nightingales 154
Dixon, "Big" Willie 19, 42
Document Records 31
Dolphy, Eric 100
Don Regon Orchestra 92
Doors, The 20
Dorsey, Jimmy 79, 109
Dorsey, Tommy 79, 106, 109

Dot Records 64
Douglas, K. C. 20
Douglas, Mike 134
Down South Boys 33
Dreamworks Records 70
Drummond, Ray 123
Drusky, Roy 72
Duckett, Slim 141
Duke Records 38, 102
Duke/Peacock Records 90
Durham, Eddie 109
Dutch Gramophone 123
Dylan, Bob 16

E

Eager, Allan 111
Earth, Wind and Fire 24
Eastwood, Clint 67, 122
Eaton, Cleveland 107
Echols, Charles 100
Eckstine, Billy 107, 108
ECM Records 113
Ecuador Chamber Orchestra 54
Eddie Vinson Sextet 102
Edsel Records 135
Edwards, David "Honeyboy" 20
Edwards, Dennis 154
Edwards, Meredith 133
Edwards, Teddy/Babe Ruth 101, 104
Elektra/Musician 99
Ellington label 111
Ellington, Duke 55, 102, 111
Ellington, Mercer 111
Ellis, Herb 100
Elvis (see Presley, Elvis)
Elzy, Ruby 44
Enanem Records 100
Engel, Lehman 125, 126
Entertainers, The 75
Epic Records 109, 151
Eschenbach, Christoph 47
Esso Trinidad Steel Band 135
Estes, Roy 158
Estes, Sleepy John 42
Everest Records 72
Everett, Betty 161

F

Fair, Archie 29
Fame, Georgie 99
Famous Door Records 106, 123
Fantastic Four 103
Fantasy Records 111, 150
Fat Cat Jazz Records 112
Fat Possum Records 28
Federal Records 17
Feilder, Alvin 102
Ferris, William 9, 39
Fields, Ernie 102
Fischer, Carl 49
Fitzgerald, Ella 101, 102, 104, 107, 109, 113

INDEX • 172

Five Blind Boys of Mississippi 17, **89**
Five Breezes, The 19
Flatt, Lester 79
Flint Symphony 49
Florentine Opera 44
Floyd, Pink 110
Flying Burrito Brothers 60
Flying Dutchman Records 100
Forbert, Steve 63
Ford, Frankie 139
Ford, Joseph 90
Ford, Tennessee Ernie 128
Fordice, Pat 93
Foster, Al 123
Foster, Frank 113
Fountain, Pete 99
Four Brothers label 146
Four Jumps of Jive 19
Four Tops, The 151
Foxx, Redd 132
Frank Capp/Nat Pierce Juggernaut 101
Franklin, Aretha 104, 121
Frederick Brothers 106
Free Lance Entertainment 133
Futura 102
Future Records 147

G

Gaines, Lee 101
Galaxy Records 109
Gants, The 161
Garland, Hank 99
Garner, Errol 98
Gary Morris Publishing 65
Gasparo Records 50
Gaye, Marvin 102
Gees 140
Genes 25
Gentry, Bobbie 64, 79
Gershwin, George 45
Getz, Stan 111, 117, 122
Giant Records 63
Gibbs, Teddy 106
Gill, Vince 67
Gillespie, Dizzy 104, 116
Gilley, Mickey 60, **64**, 67
Gilmer, Will 68
Gilmore, Jimmie Dale 61
Gilmore, John 102
Gleason, Jackie 106
Glenn Miller Band 128
Glenn, Scott 61
Glover, Danny 27
Golden Crest Records 109
Goldovsky Opera 44, 57
Goldsboro, Bobby 151
Golia, Vinny 100
Goodman, Benny 101, 106, 109
Gordon, Dexter 102, 117
Gordon, Jerry 102
Gordon, Jim 159
Gospel and Religious 85
Graham, Clay 93

Graham, Cleve 93
Graham, Elgie 93
Graham, Glen 158
Graham, Theophilles 93
Granz, Norman 116
Grateful Dead 20
Graves, Blind Roosevelt 141
Gray, John 107
Gray, Wardell 102
Green, Al 151
Green, Lillian "Lil" 21
Greenfield, Elizabeth Taylor 46
Griffin, Dick 102
Griffin, Johnny 111
Griffin, Merv 134
Griffith, Andy 61
Grove Boys 150
GSF 151
Guild Records 108
Gulf Coast Symphony 53
Guthrie, Arlo 135
Guy and Davis 134

H

Hackett, Bobby 106
Hadley, Dardanelle 103
Haggard, Merle 16
Hall, Daryl 154
Hallyday, Johnny 136
Hampton Records 111
Hampton, Lionel 99, 111, 113
Handy, W. C. 10, 55
Hanson, Howard 48
Harmony Boys 150
Harper's Bizarre 134
Harrington, Eddie 17
Harris, Coot 149
Harris, Emmylou 78
Harris, Joel Chandler 135
Harris, William 141
Harris, Wyonnie 102
Harrison, George 136
Hart, Freddie 60
Hassan, Ali 102
Hatchett, Monroe 93
Hawkins, Coleman 108
Hawkins, Emmit 138
Hayes, Helen 126
Henderson, Fletcher 107, 116
Henderson, Michael 103
Hendricks, Scott 65
Hendrix, Jimi 24, 39
Herbie Holmes Orchestra 106
Herman's Hermits 139
Herman, Woody 109
Herring, Sid 162
Herrington, Benjamin 46
Hess, Jake 88
Heyward, DuBose 45
Hi label 161
Hibbler, Al 104
Hicks, Bobby 63
High Note label 102
Highsteppers 165

Hill, Andrew 113
Hill, Faith 65
Hill, Tyrone 102
Hill, Z. Z. 23, 30, 139
Hill,Andrew 102
Hillery, Art 104
Hilliard Music Enterprise 47
Hilliard, Quincy 47
Hines, Earl 102
Hines, Frank 116
Hinton, Milt 104
Hirt, Al 99
Hite, Les 100, 115
Hodges, Eddie 60
Hoffman, Dustin 37
Holiday, Billie 116
Hollywood, Bo Jack 37
Holmes, Herbie 106
Holt, Redd 107
Hooker, Earl 21, 36
Hooker, John Lee 21, 34, 113, 139, **149**
Hope, Bob 134
Hopkins, Fred 100
Hopkins, Lightnin' 42
Horne, Lena 107
Horton, Big Walter 20
Horton, Walter "Shakey" 22
House, Eddie James "Son" 22, 27, 33, 35, 39, 41, 141
Houston Grand Opera 57
Houston Symphony 49
Hovis, Guy 134
Howard, Harlan 60, 62
Howlin' Wolf (see Burnett, Chester Arthur "Howlin' Wolf")
Hubbard, Freddie 102, 111
Hughes, Bill 50
Humphries, Lex 102
Hunter, Tab 72
Hurt, "Mississippi" John 16, **23**, 25
Hutson, Nancy 106

I

Iceland Symphony 49
Imbragoulio, John V. 138
Import label 104
Impressions 161
Impulse label 102
Induction Gala 167
Ingram, James 120
International Submarine Band 60
International Sweethearts of Rhythm 107
Irving, Washington 13
Ives, Burl 78

J

Jackson Harmoneers, The 90
Jackson Southernaires, The 24, **90**, 92

Jackson, Alan 65
Jackson, Eddie 89
Jackson, James 102
Jackson, Michael 121
Jackson, Milt 104
Jackson, Vasti 23
Jacksons, The 102
Jagger, Mick 136
James Blackwood Quartet 86
James, Elmore 18, **24**, 28, 34, 42
James, Nehemiah "Skip" 25, 39, 141
Jan & Dean 135
Jarvis, John 71
Jarvis,Clifford 102
Jazz 97
Jazz Messengers 102
JCOA 113
Jenkins, Harold Lloyd 80
Jennings, Luther 90
Jennings, Waylon 60, 72
Jimmie Lunceford Band 115
Jive/Novus Records 111
JMT records 115
JMT/Verve label 115
John, Elton 120
Johnson, J. J. 99
Johnson, Jimmy 67
Johnson, Lonnie 42
Johnson, Luther "Guitar Junior" 25, 141
Johnson, Pete 98
Johnson, President Lyndon 53
Johnson, Robert 11, 15, 19, 20, 22, 23, 24, 25, **27**, 33, 34, 39, 42, 141
Johnson, Tommy 10, **28**, 35, 141
Johnson, Willie 93
Johnson, Willie Neal 91
Jones, Bill 63
Jones, Casey 141
Jones, Dallas 68
Jones, Eddie "Guitar Slim" 139, **149**
Jones, Elvin 113
Jones, Floyd 21, 28
Jones, George 67, 72, 84
Jones, Hank 102, **108**
Jones, Laurence C. 107
Jones, "Little" Johnny 28
Jones, Quincy 120, 121
Jones, Samuel 48
Joplin, Scott 57, 103
Jordan, Louis 98
Jordan,Clifford 102
Jordonaires, The 138
Jubes, The 93
Judd, Naomi 71
Judds, The 71

K

Kabell Records 113
Kane, Candye 135

Kansas City Red 21
Kendrick, Eddie 154
Kennedy, President John 147
Kennedy, Tiny 140
Kenton, Stan 112, 115, 122
Kessel, Barney 100
Kimbrough, Junior 28
King Biscuit Boys, The 36
King Biscuit Entertainers 42
King Oliver 100, 116
King, Albert 38, 149, **150**
King, B. B. 18, 23, **29**, 31, 34, 38, 97, 119, 150-151, 155
King, Evelyn "Champagne" 121
King, Riley B. 29
Kirk, Andy 99, 108, 116
Kirk, Rahsaan Roland 113
Knights, The 67
Knobloch, Fred 67
Koch Records 64
Kondor, Robbie 63
Konnex Records 103
Kotick, Teddy 99
Kravitz, Lenny 152

L

Lake George Opera 44, 57
Landmark Records 111
Lane, James A. 38
Lang, Eddie 112
LaRoca, Pete 102
LaSalle Records 17
LaSalle, Denise 24, **30**, 139
Latimore 30
Laughton, Charles 126
Lazarowitz, Barry 63
League/ISCM 54
Leake County Revelers 68
Led Zeppelin 27
LeDoux, Chris 69
Lee, Brenda 71
Lee, George 116
Lee, Peggy 21, 101, 122, 128
Lee, Tommy 138
Lennon, John 122, 136
Leno, Jay 152
Lert, Richard 49
Les and Larry Elgart Band 128
Letterman, David 65, 109
Lewis, Bobby 147
Lewis, Jerry Lee 16, 64, 67, 72, 161, **162**, 165
Lewis, Ramsey 107
Liberty label 19
Liberty Records 62, 69, 162
Lightfoot, Gordon 135
Linkletter, Art 134
Lippman, Horst 42
Liston, Melba 115
Little Boy Blue 42
Little Brother 39
Little Feat 135
Little Milton (see Campbell, Little Milton)

Littlejohn, Johnny 140
Lockwood, Robert "Junior" 42
Logan, Joshua 126
Lomax, Alan 9, 21, 22, 23, 31, 33
Lombardo, Guy 106
London Philharmonic Orchestra, The 72
London Records 158
Lorvin, Charlie 79
Los Angeles Philharmonic Orchestra 115
Lott, Trent 134
Louis Armstrong All Stars 104, 112
Louis, Joe Hill 155
Louisville Orchestra 54
Lowe, Mundell 110, **122**, 128
Luandrew, "Sunnyland Slim" Albert 31
Lucious, Roscoe 89
Lunceford, Jimmie 109
Lyles, Bill 88
Lynn, Loretta 78, 82
Lyon, Patricia 67
Lyons, Bobby 158

M

Mabley, Moms 132
Mabus, Governor Ray 78
Machito 111
Machlis, Joseph 9
Madden, Kenneth 93
Maghett, "Good Rocking Sam"/ "Magic Sam" 31
Magic Rockers 25
Magic Slim 141
Magnolia Records 138
Malaco Records 30, 31, 32, 90, 91, 92, 94, **139**, 151
Malkovich, John 136
Malone, Tom 109
Malouf, Mitchell 139
Mandrell, Barbara 30, 62
Manhattan Transfer 135
Maphis, Joe 60
Maranatha Music 93
March, Frederic 126
Marsalis, Branford 111
Marsalis, Ellis 100
Marsalis, Wynton 23
Martin, Mary 46
Martyn, Barry 100
Mase, Ray 54
Mashboro Records 93
Mason, Dave 159
Masters V, The 86
Mat Britt Orchestra 111
Mathis, Johnny 106
Mathis, Samantha 61
Max Roach-Clifford Brown Quintet 102
Mayall, John 98
Mays, Bill 123

MCA 15, 30, 80, 120
McAnally, Mac 69
McClennan, Tommy 20, **31**
McCoy, Charlie 16, **31**, 32, 141
McCracken, Dr. C. C. 45
McDaniel, Ellas 147
McDonald, Hugh 63
McDowell, "Mississippi" Fred 16, **31**
McDowell, Bonnie 31
McEntire, Reba 65
McGhee, Howard 102
McGraw, Tim 67
McGuire, Barry 93
McKinley, Ray 122
McMurray, Lillian 24, 138, **140**
McMurray, Willard 140
McRae, Carmen 113
McWilliams, Elsie 70
McWilliams, Skeets 110
Melrose, Lester 18
Memphis Recording Service 155
Memphis Slim 39, 113
Mercury Records 19, 81, 107, 109, 162
Meridian Arts Ensemble 47
Metropolitan Opera 44, 47, 53
MGM 81, 134
Midland-Odessa Symphony 49
Mighty Sparrow 135
Mili, Gjon 116
Miller, Aleck Ford "Rice" 41
Miller, Jody 72
Miller, Mulgrew 111, 115
Miller, Roger 60
Miller, Walter 102
Milsap, Ronnie 62
Milton, Roy 102
Mingus, Charlie 101
Miracle Records 154
Mission City Playboys 61
Mississippi Mass Choir 90, **91**, 92, 139
Mississippi Mud Steppers 33
Mississippi Music Heritage Museum 167
Mississippi Sheiks 16, 17, **32**, 40, 141
Mississippi Show Stoppers 132
Mitchell, Guy 128
MMB 54
Mo'tet 100
Mobley, Mary Ann 128
Moe and the Mavericks 61
Mojo Men 134
Monaural Records 109
Monica 152
Montgomery, Little Brother 19
Montgomery, Vince 162
Monument Records 72
Moody, James 107
Mooney, Ralph 72
Moore, Dorothy 139, **151**

Moore, Dudley 136
Moore, Milton Aubrey "Brew" 111
Morganfield, McKinley 33
Morganfield, "Muddy Waters" **33**, 36, 39, 42, 149
Morissette, Alanis 121
Morris, Butch 113
Morrison, Van 98, 99
Mosley, R. O. 68
Moten, Bennie 116
Motion Pictures 119
Motown 103, 153, 155, 166
Movin' On Productions 153
Muddy Waters (see Morganfield, "Muddy Waters")
Mugge, Robert 27
Mullen, Moon 111
Mulligan, Gerry 111
Murry, David 100
Muscle Shoals 70
Muse Records 102, 109
Music Corporation of America 106
Musical Theater 125
Musselwhite, Charlie 34
Myers, Sam 34

N

'N Sync 132
Nabors, Jim 134
Nance, Teddy 102
Narvo, Red 106
Naxos Records 49
NBC-TV Opera Company 51
Nelson, Albert 150
Nelson, Oliver 101
Nelson, Ricky 72
Nelson, Tracy 72
Nelson, Willie 62
Nemperor Records 63
Nettles, Isaiah 141
New Air 115
New Haven Symphony 44, 47
New Kids On The Block 132
New Orleans Philharmonic 49
New Rose Records 15
New World Records 138
New York Brass Quintet 47
New York Opera 44
New York Philharmonic 57
New York Trumpet Ensemble 47
Newman, David 100
Newman, Randy 134
Nighthawk, Robert 36
Nitty Gritty Dirt Band 165
Nordine, Ken 107
Norwood, Brandy 151
Norwood, Pig 141

O

O'Neal, Jim 140
Oates, John 154

Ochs, Phil 135
OKeh Records 23, 33, 41, 107, 141
Oliver, Sy 109, 115
Omoe, Eloe 102
Onderdock, David 107
Onyx Records 102
Opera Ebony 44
Opera South 44, 57
Orbison, Roy 62, 67, 261
Original Jazz Records 102, 111
Osby, Greg 115
Oslin, K. T. 61
Osmond Brothers, The 67
Osmond, Marie 63
Ovation 19
Overstreet, Paul 63, **70**
Owens, Buck 60, 78
Owens, Buddy 93
Owens, Jimmy 92

P

Pablo Records 117
Page, Hot Lips 108
Page, Jimmy 38, 42
Page, Patti 78
Palmer, Robert 28
Palmer, Willard 50
Paramount 14, 41, 141
Parham, Tiny 104
Parker, Charlie 102, 117
Parker, Colonel Tom 165
Parker, Herman 34
Parker, Little Junior 34
Parks, Van Dyke 134
Parnassus 54
Parsons, Gram 60
Parton, Dolly 67, 78
Pass, Joe 100
Patton, Charlie 10, 21, 22, 23, 27, 28, **35**, 41, 141
Paul English Traveling Show 111
Pauley, Roy 88
Paycheck, Johnny 62, 82
Peacock-Songbird Records 93
Peavey Electronics 140
Peavey, Hartley 140
Peck Kelly's Jazz Band 111
Peebles, Ann 30
Peg Leg Sam 149
Pendergrass, Teddy 121
Pepper, Allen 134
Perkins, Carl 161
Perkins, Joe Willie "Pinetop" 36, 42
Perkins, Percell 90
Perry, Audrey Faith 65
Peters, Ben 71
Petway, Robert 20
Philadelphia Orchestra 49, 57
Phillips Country Ramblers 81
Phillips, Sam 11, 36, 155, 161, 162, 165
Philwood label 28
Phoenix, River 61

Pickett, Wilson 151
Pilgrim Jubilees, The 93
Pillow, Ray 72
Piney Woods School 90, 107
Pitts, Clyde 71
Pittsburgh Symphony 49
Plantation Music Orchestra 115
Pointblank Records 94
PolyGram Records 147
Pope John Paul II 92
Poppies, The 151
Popular (Pop) 131
Porcino, Al 115
Porter, Cole 134
Prague Symphony 49
Presley, Elvis 10, 11, 18, 20, 34, 81, 82, 85, 119, 128, 157, **163**
Prestige Records 99
Preston, Billy 103
Preston, Don 100
Price, Mary Violet Leontyne 51
Price, Ray 62, 72
Pride, Charley 67, 71, **72**, 73
Priester, Julian 102
Primal Press 54
Production 137
Promotion 137
Pugh, Virginia Wynette 82

Q

Queen Victoria 46
Quest Records 120
Quicksilver Recording Co. 38
Quinn, Edwin McIntosh "Snoozer" 111

R

Ra, Sun 102
Rachell, Yank 20
Radio City Orchestra 113
Raitt, Bonnie 98
Raspberry, Larry 165
Ravin' Blue Band 67
Rawls, Lou 72, 99, 100, 101, 102, 151
Ray Anthony Band 110
Ray, Michael 102
RCA 71, 72, 73, 101, 109, 154
RCA Victor 75, 77, 88, 103, 108, 146
RCA/Bluebird 18
Reagan, President Ronald 53
Recording 137
Red Cap Orchestra 111
Red Counts, The 138
Red Lightnin' Records 18, 166
Reed, Jerry 67
Reed, Mathis James "Jimmy" 39, 150, **153**
Reeves, Jim 78
Rejoice Records 151

Revelation Records 100
Reynolds, Blind Joe 141
Reynolds, Burt 67, 84
Rhino Records 162
Rhythm and Blues 145
Rich, Charlie 139
Richardson, Rick 138
Rick and the Rockets 138
Rimes, Margaret LeAnn 74
Risen Star Fife and Drum Band, The 40
Rivers, Johnny 22
Riverside Records 21
Roach, Max 113
Robbins, Marty 62
Roberson, Major 93
Roberts, Gaylen 134
Roberts, Julia 67
Robinson, Bobby 18
Robinson, Fenton 36
Robinson, Stevie 147
Robison, Williard 112
Rochester Opera 44
Rochester Philharmonic 49, 56
Rock and Roll 157
Rodgers, Andy 36
Rodgers, Jesse 77
Rodgers, Jimmie 10, 11, 59, 70, **75**, 77, 141
Rogers, Bernard 48
Rogers, Jimmy 22, **38**
Rogers, Kenny 60, 71
Rogers, Leland 60
Rolling Stones, The 10, 98, 99, 122, 136, 149
Rolling Stones, Andy Anderson and 138, **158**
Rollins, Sonny 113
Roman, Tony 136
Ronstadt, Linda 78
Roosevelt, Eleanor 46
Rooster Blues Records 18, **140**
Roosters, The 161
Rosetta Records 108
Ross, Charles Isaiah "Doc" 38
Ross, Diana 110, 153, 166
Rouse, Steve 53
RSO Records 155
Rubinstein, Arthur, Jr. 135
Ruffin Brothers 155
Ruffin, David 153, **154**
Ruffin, Jimmy 153, **154**
Rufus and Bones 155
Rush, "Little" Otis 31, **38**, 150
Rush, Bobby 24
Russell, Jane 128
Russell, Johnny 78
Russell, Leon 159
Rydell, Bobby 106

S

Sackville Records 113
Saginaw Symphony 49

Sammy Kaye Band 128
Sanborn, David 64
Sanders, Sonny 147
San Francisco Opera 53
SAR 146
Satellite Records 155
Saunders, Red 101
Savoy Records 94, 109, 111
Sawyer Brown 70
Saxton, Bob 78, 110
Schlitz, Don 71
Schubert, Kathleen L. 50
Schuyler, Knobloch & Overstreet 68
Schwarz, Gerard 49, 54
Sclater, James 54
Scorcese, Martin 80
Sears, Al 116
Seattle Symphony 49
Second Chapter of Acts 93
Seeley, Jeannie 72
Sequel label 104
Sessions, Roger 126
Severinsen, Doc 109, 122
Sharp, Martha 65
Shaw, Artie 109
Shaw, Eddie 140
Shaw, Woody 111
Shea, George Beverly 93
Shenandoah 70
Sherrill, Billy 82
Shields, Lonnie 140
Shore, Dinah 134
Shrill, Billy 60
Sidlin. Murry 44
Silberschlag, Jeff 54
Sills, Beverly 44
Simms Twins 146
Simon, Carly 135
Simon, George 109
Simon, Paul 110
Sims, Zoot 111
Sinatra, Frank 122
Sioux City Symphony 49
Slay, Emitt 112
Smith, Brad 158
Smith, Carl 72
Smith, Connie 65, 72, 80
Smith, Dalton 112
Smith, Huey 138
Smith, James 149
Smith, Jimmy 99
Smith, Johnny 100
Smith, Sonelius Larel 112
Smith, Wadada Leo 112
Smith, Willie 109, 115
Snoden, Elmer 109
Snow, Donnie 11
Snowden, Don 20
Sonet Records 111
Songbird label 95
Sony 16
Soul 145
Soul Records 154, 155
Soul Stirrers 146

Sound Solutions 15
Southern Funk 155
Southern Gospel Singers 92
Southern Sons Quartet 140
Southerners Gospel Quartet 138
Spann, Otis 36, **39**, 42
Specialty Records 146
Speir, H. C. 10, 68, 75, 137, **141**
St. Andrews Gospelaires 140
St. Louis Symphony 54
St. Therese 110
Stabulas, Nick 99
Stafford, Greg 100
Stafford, Jim 64
Stampley, Joe 61
Stan Kenton Orchestra 122
Staple Singers, The 94
Staples, Cleotha 94
Staples, Mavis 94
Staples, Roebuck "Pops" 94
Staples, Yvonne 94
Starr, Ringo 78, 135, 136
Statler Brothers, The 78
Stax Records 32, 150, 155, 165
Steeple Chase Records 111
Steinberg, William 49
Stephenson, Wolf 139
Steve Miller Band 20
Stevens, Ray 67, 139
Stevens, Thomas Roger 158
Stewart, Jimmy 64
Stewart, Lisa 79
Stewart, Prince 99
Stewart, Wynn 72
Stigers, Curtis 121
Still, William Grant 55
Stills, Stephen 134
Stone, Judy 147
Storyville Records 111
Strait, George 78, 121
Strata-East Records 113
Streisand, Barbra 106, 121
Stuart, Marty 79
Stubberfield, John 113
Stuckey, Nat 72
Sugar Hill label 79
Sullivans, The 79
Sumlin, Hubert 39
Summer, Donna 112
Summit Records 54
Sun Records 11, 15, 34, 38, 155, 161, 163
Sun Records. 162
Sundazed Records 162
Sunset Records 138
Supremes, The 166
Surrell, Maurice 90
Swallow, John 46
Swan, Jimmy 60
Swing Thing 100
Swinging Gold Coasters 14
Sykes, Roosevelt 39

T

Tallent, Garry 63
Tampa Red 18, 19
Taylor, Dublow 42
Taylor, Eddie "Playboy" 39, 153
Taylor, Greg "Fingers" 67, 160, **165**
Taylor, Johnnie 23
Taylor, Johnny 139, 146
Taylor, Theodore Roosevelt "Hound Dog" 39
Television 119
Temple, Johnnie "Geechie" 21, **39**
Temptations, The 154
Terry, Gordon 72
Thirteen Original Blue Devils, The 116
Thomas Trio, The 138
Thomas, B. J. 68
Thomas, Elvie 141
Thomas, James "Son" 39
Thomas, Rufus 155
Thompson, Theo 89
Thomson, Virgil 44, 51
Thornton, Big Mama 18, 99
Thornton, Billy Bob 80
Threadgill, Henry 115
Three Dog Night 112
Tillis, Pam 61
Timeless label 102
Tina and the Tides 138
Today's Artists, Inc. 44
Tomato Records 162
Towels, Nat 99
Townshend, Pete 99
Travis, Randy 70, 84
Travolta, John 37
Tritt, Travis 80
Trumpet Records 24, 42, 138, 140
Tubb, Ernest 70
Tubb, Joe 158
Tucker, Tanya 62, 63
Tunnell, Michael 54
Turnbull, Dr. Walter 57
Turner, Ike 15, 18, 32, 42, **156**, 159
Turner, Othar 40
Turner, Tina 156
Twitty, Conway 62, 72, **80**
Tyner, McCoy 102, 113

U

Utah Symphony 49
Utica Jubilee Singers 19, **95**

V

Vaccaro, Brenda 61
Vanguard 25, 34
Vaughan, Stevie Ray 38, 150
Vee, Bobby 134
Vee-Jay label 101
Verity Records 89
Verve Records 102, 123
Vick, H. 113
Victor 14, 62, 112, 141
Vincent, Gene 72
Vincent, Johnny 138
Vinson, Eddie "Cleanhead" 99
Vinson, Walter 32, **40**
Vinton, Bobby 62, 78
Vocalion 41
Vogue Records 15
Volt Records 151

W

Wagner, Jack 121
Waits, Freddie 113
Walker, Billy 79
Walker, Charley 72
Walker, Robert 140
Wallace, Jerry 72
Walton, Cedar 100
Wardlow, Gayle Dean 10, 143
Warner Brothers 23, 109, 123, 135, 154
Warner Mack 138
Washboard Walter 141
Watkins, Cornelius Dwayne 89
Watkins, Harvey, Jr. 89
Watkins, Harvey, Sr. 89
Watson, Gene 78
Watts, Andre 101
Wea Records 146
Weatherspoon, Jimmy 99
Webb, Carol 92
Webster, Ben 104
Webster, Katie 23
Weede, Robert 44
Weir, Tommy 112
Welk, Lawrence 106
Wellington, Valerie 141
Wells, Carlton 138
Wells, Lloyd 110, **128**
West, Dottie 62, 72, 78
Westbound Records 30
White, Booker T. Washington "Bukka" 41
White, Chris 107
White, Dr. Michael 99
Whiteman, Paul 55, 109, 111, 112
Whiteman, Wilberforce 109
Whitman, Slim 72
Who, The 98, 139
Wiggins, Jerry 60
Wiggs label 112
Wiggs, Johnny 111
Wilberforce University String Quartet 55
Wilcox, Eddie 109
Wilderson, Ed 101
Wiley, Cheeshie 141
Wilkins, Robert Timothy 41, 141

Williams Brothers, The 24, **95**, 138
Williams, Joe Lee "Big Joe" 20, 35, **41**, 42, 140
Williams, Frank 91, 92, 95
Williams, Huey 90
Williams, Joe 104, 113
Williams, Joe Lee 41
Williams, Leon "Pop" 95
Williams, Leonard 95
Williams, Melvin 95
Williams, R. E. 40
Williams, Tony 111
Williamson, Sonny Boy 18, 19, 29, **41**, 138, 140, 156
Wills, Bob and the Texas Playboys 37
Wilrich, Jack 111
Wilson Phillips 121
Wilson, Brian 134
Wilson, Cassandra 113
Wilson, Christine 9
Wilson, Flip 132
Wilson, Gerald Stanley 101, 102, 113, **115**
Wilson, Jackie 150
Wilson, John 103
Wilson, Mary 166
Winding, Kai 111, 122
Winter, Johnny 24, 98
Winter, Paul 113
Wolverton, Jim 68
Wonder, Stevie 103
Wood, Chris 149
Wood, Don 162
Woodard, Lloyd 90
Workman, Nanette 135
Wray, Bob 64
Wyman, Bill 99
Wynette, Linda and Imogene 82
Wynette, Tammy 59, 67, 72, **82**

Y

Yamboo label 19
Yancey's Band 150
Yardbirds, The 22, 42, 149
Yearwood, Trisha 61
Young, El Dee 107
Young, Faron 72
Young, John O. "Johnny" 42
Young, Lee 116
Young, Lester 90, 109, **116**
Young, Neil 62
Young, Patsy 112
Young, Snooky 115

Z

Zaninelli, Luigi 53
Zappa, Frank 47
Zinermon, Ike 27

INDEX • 176